FOOTPRINTS
ON THE PATH

I was shown a path with footprints on it, and I heard the words, 'Follow thou Me.'

Sometimes that path was straight and smooth. At other times it was rough, very winding and difficult. At times the footprints seemed to disappear completely when there were obstacles to be overcome.

I still heard the words, 'Follow thou Me. Be not concerned when there are obstacles, for every obstacle that is overcome strengthens your faith and belief in Me, your constant guide and companion.'

Other books by Eileen Caddy

The Dawn of Change
God Spoke to Me
Flight into Freedom
Foundations of a Spiritual Community
The Living Word
Opening Doors Within

Video tape:
Opening Doors Within

FOOTPRINTS
ON THE PATH

Eileen Caddy

edited and compiled by
Roy McVicar

Findhorn Press

We would like to make it clear that the Findhorn Community
referred to in this book is not the local Scottish village of
Findhorn but the community that has grown up around the
Findhorn Foundation.

Copyright © Eileen Caddy 1976
First published 1976
Reprinted 1979
Second edition 1981
Reprinted 1985, 1987, 1988
Third edition 1991

ISBN 0 905249 80 1

Illustrated by Jane Crosen
Cover illustration © Lawry Gold
Author photograph by Findhorn Foundation Visual Arts
Layout by Claudia Klingemann, Bay Area Graphics
Set in Palatino on Macintosh SE
Printed and bound by Wheatons Ltd, Exeter, UK
Published by Findhorn Press, The Park, Findhorn,
Forres IV36 0TZ, Moray, Scotland

Printed on oxygen-bleached 'environmentally friendly' paper

Contents

Introduction to the Third Edition   7

Introduction to the First Edition   9

Awareness   11

Change   51

Oneness   91

Service   131

Nutshells   171

Footprints in snow,
Footprints in snow.
Where do you come from,
Where do you go?

*— from a poem by Stephen Field
which befriended the illustrations*

Introduction to the Third Edition

Over the thirty years of its existence and growth the
Findhorn Foundation, and now the wider Community
around it, has been remarkably open to all ideas and teachings, new and old, which make a contribution to living a
more aware and spiritual life and creating a better world.
All these philosophies have much to offer, and yet with the
passing of time and the continuing advent of increasingly
sophisticated and complex spiritual theories and 'new age'
techniques, it becomes more and more obvious that the simple and direct teaching that has come through Eileen Caddy
forms an absolutely solid basis for living a practical sacred
life. The very simplicity of this teaching is what makes it
stand out among the growing clutter of the new age mar-
ketplace.

Eileen has gone through a long process of change in rela-
tion to her 'voice within'. When she first became aware of it
during the 1950s, and for some years afterwards, it
addressed her as 'my beloved child' and spoke to her as
does a loving father. After a while the relationship changed
and the voice began to address her as 'my beloved'. In
recent years Eileen has come to realise that in regarding the
voice as something outside herself she was separating herself from God. 'God is within,' she says now, 'therefore I am
the voice.' As she looks back over the guidance she has
received over the years, she sees that again and again she
was told: 'We are one; there is no separation.' It took her
several years, though, to experience this as a reality in her
own life.

Much of Eileen's guidance, some of it containing very
specific instructions, was received for the community as a
whole during its early years and was undeniably valuable
in guiding the fledgling centre along the right path. Yet at a
certain point Eileen stopped receiving guidance for others,
as her 'voice' insisted that in the long run this was not
healthy. Indeed, Eileen believes that the most valuable way

to help others is to turn them inwards to their own spiritual resources, and her work now centres around this task. This presents a striking contrast with the modern trend towards 'channelling' supposedly lofty beings—of often dubious credentials—who sometimes seem to expect to be obeyed unquestioningly.

Footprints on the Path contains gentle but direct messages of the kind which are most likely to turn the reader inside towards his or her own divine source. Eileen sees this book as containing a complete teaching in how to live a spiritual life, and the reader can either follow it step by step or dip into it at random. We trust that each individual will discover how they can use it best.

Sandra Kramer, Findhorn Press

Introduction to the First Edition

The inspirational writings in this book had their origin as
Eileen Caddy, co-founder of the Findhorn Community, lis-
tened to the voice of the God within. Many years ago that
voice had come to her at a time of great uncertainty and
unhappiness, and through the years it has been her constant guide and stimulus and hope.

The messages here offer, to those who will read them
receptively, nothing less than a way of living which can be
more meaningful, more purposeful, and result in a more
worthwhile contribution to life.

They may be deceptive in their simplicity. If you look in
them for either beautiful spiritual sentiments or profound
philosophical truths, you will miss their real value for you
and in so doing you will miss a wealth of life and love and
wisdom.

For their very simplicity can be their greatest challenge.
No matter how advanced you may be on the spiritual path,
there is on every page, almost in every line, a challenge con-
cerning your way of life, your way of living, the actual
expression or demonstration of your inward spiritual state.

The messages cannot be classified, for they are living
truths which are as complex and varied as life itself. They
should therefore not be read like ordinary devotional talks
or sermonettes because they are not these. There is only one
way in which to read them, and that is first to make up
your mind that either they are in fact how Eileen has picked
up what God was saying to her and through her, or else
they are not worth your time to read. But if you can be open
to their divine origin, then they can be a unique and wonderful thing for you: they can be as a mirror in which to
look at yourself.

Read each sentence as being spoken to you, and apply-
ing to you. See where it does apply, and what steps you can
then take in the light of what it has shown.

If you will do this, taking the messages one at a time,

then each one can open another window in your soul towards eternity. Each one will enable you to make your life richer and fuller and happier and more effective in service. Each one will be another step towards realising some of your fondest hopes for your own life, and even more important towards attaining the highest potential of which you are capable—God's supreme purpose for your life.

In other words, these messages can be as 'footprints on the path' which lead you home to God.

Roy McVicar

AWARENESS

I was aware of a tremendous increase of light. It seemed to spread out gradually like the glorious sunrise.

I heard the words: 'My light is always there. Become more and more aware of it and of its full power and glory.'

Then I saw before me in great letters of fire the word AWARENESS.

Wake up and live.

Set your sights high,
the higher the better.
Expect the most wonderful things to happen,
not in the future but right now.
Realise that nothing is too good.
Allow absolutely nothing to hamper you
or hold you up in any way.

Be enthusiastic about life.
It is a wonderful life;
make it so by your enthusiasm.

Learn to be very clear and definite
about what you desire in life;
never be vague or uncertain.
You can do all things,
you can be all things to all people
when your faith and trust are in Me.
Have confidence in your ability to do all things
because you are drawing your substance,
your all, from Me.
I am your all in all.

Stride forward with a firm, steady step,
knowing with a deep, certain inner knowing
that you will reach every goal you set yourself,
that you will achieve every aim.

Start doing this today.
Why put off until tomorrow

what you know you can do today?
Far too many souls procrastinate
or suffer from inertia,
with the result that nothing gets done;
and they go on vaguely hoping
that one day something will happen to change
       their lives,
that perhaps circumstances will take a hand,
and then everything will fall into place for them.
It is not the way to live a full and glorious life—
in a vague and dreaming fashion.

Why not take positive action?
Why not start the wheels turning?
Once you have done your part
you will receive all the help you need,
but not until then.
I help those who help themselves,
not those who sit back hoping that something
       will happen
but fail to take any action.

You can soar to great heights
with hearts filled with praise and thanksgiving;
but like the tiny lark, you have to take off from the
       ground,
you have to make that special effort.
It need not be a strain,
it can be a joyous light-hearted effort
which is an effortless effort.

Once you are off the ground
up and up you can go with complete freedom.
Why remain anchored
when action on your part can change your life
       completely?

When you desire something badly enough
you will achieve it:
you will allow nothing to stand in the way,
you will never take 'no' for an answer
but will know you can do all things with Me.

The take-off of an aeroplane from the ground
demands a special boost of power.
Go within and receive your special boost of power
to set you on your way.

There is no greater power than My power
and it is available to you
at any time
when you choose to draw from it.
I never withhold it from any who are ready
who reach out for it
and use it aright.

It is yours
when you are ready.

You are surrounded by beauty everywhere.
Open your eyes
and see it
and give constant thanks for it.

Let the things of beauty transform you and inspire you
to your highest and best.
Beauty draws the very best out of and unites you
with the highest.

The beauty that is within you cannot be contained . . . .
it will be reflected without;
let it shine forth.
Fill your heart and mind with beautiful thoughts
and reflect Me
for I am beauty.

Look for the beauty in everything,
and when you look deep enough and long enough
you will see it.
Rise above the sordid ugly things in life,
for by rising above them
you can help to transform and transmute them.
Beauty is in the eye of the beholder,
therefore it is deep within you.
Go forth this day determined to see beauty
in everyone and everything
and you will do so.

Love and beauty go hand in hand.
So let My universal love flow freely in and through
each one of you,
bringing unity and oneness.
As each one of you opens your heart
and keeps the love flowing
this will come about;
for the more love there is between all of you
the greater will be the unity and oneness.

I say to you over and over again, 'Love one another.'
This does not mean that you are to tolerate one another,
or try very hard to love one another;
but you will find when you open your hearts
and can fill them with loving, beautiful thoughts
that you will want to love
all those you come into contact with
no matter who they are.

16

This is the free flow of My universal love
which knows no discrimination
and does not pick and choose who is going to be loved
and who is not.
My love is the same for each and every one.
How much you are willing to accept is up to you.

You can be infilled by My wondrous love,
or you can shut it out of your lives;
it is simply up to you.
It is always there waiting for you when you are
        ready for it.

This is what is taking place at this time.
There is a wonderful opening up and acceptance of
        My love
which brings you all closer together,
uniting you in oneness.

Be not afraid to express this love;
it is beyond the personality,
it is of the very highest.

There is nothing possessive about it,
for a possessive love stifles and kills;
it shuts out My divine love.
My universal love grows and grows.
It includes everyone,
it possesses no one,
and yet all are one in it,
all feel part of it.
It enfolds all because it is the allness of all—all inclusive.

Learn to wear your heart on your sleeve
and never be ashamed
to demonstrate your love for one another.

17

Love is the greatest uniting factor in the universe,
so love, love, love.

Raise your consciousness.
Realise that you are ageless,
you are as young as time,
as old as eternity.
As you live fully and gloriously in the ever-present now,
you are always as young as the present,
you are constantly being reborn in spirit and in truth.

You cannot remain static in this spiritual life;
there is always something new and exciting
to learn and to do.
Living in a state of expectancy
keeps you ever alert and young.
When the mind becomes old and dull,
life loses all its sparkle and zest.
Keep your mind alert and you can never grow old.

The fountain of youth is your consciousness;
the joy of living is the elixir of life.

Expect the very best in life and draw it to you.
For too long so many of you have accepted this in theory,
but have failed to live it
and demonstrate it.
Why not start doing something about it right now!
Stop thinking about it and talking about it.
All the time I am urging you to live a life;
over and over again I ask you to live that life.

If you are tired of hearing the same things repeated
then why not do something about it?

Until these vitally important lessons
are absorbed by each one
and become part of you
and they live and move and have their being in you,
I have to go on repeating them.

When you teach a child to do something
you may have to show that child
the same thing many times,
you may have to wait very patiently
while it fumbles around trying to do it on its own.
The child may appear to be all thumbs,
but unless you allow it to try
it will never learn.
Simply watching you doing it all the time
will not help the child to learn for itself.
That is why life has to be lived for it to be really effective;
and you have to live it.
No one else can live your life for you.

Always be willing to learn,
to accept the new;
never close your mind and reject it
because you cannot understand it.
Open yourself up
and allow the new to reveal itself
and always be willing to go halfway.
A closed mind will get you nowhere
for you cannot grow and expand
when you close your mind.
There are always two sides to a picture;
learn to be tolerant,
try to see both sides.

'Judge not that ye be not judged';
condemn not that you be not condemned.

Be a good listener.
Everyone likes a good listener.
Unless you take time to listen to what someone has
        to say
you can be of no help to that soul.

You will find that when you fail to understand
some new truth with the mind,
if you sit still
and raise your consciousness
you will be able to get into tune
with the infinite, universal mind
and to become one with it, with Me,
and you will be able to understand all things.

Rejoice
and give constant thanks
for the best is yet to come.

Day after day
I pour down upon you all My good and perfect gifts.
You are surrounded by all the best in life.
So open your eyes
and behold My wonders
and realise how mightily blessed you are.

Cease bemoaning your lot in life,
cease concentrating on the negative things in your life;

concentrate on all the wonderful things
until they become reality
until they become part of you.

Take off those blinkers,
see the miracles of life
and realise that you are part of it,
that you live and move and have your being in it.

Why not make a habit of approaching life in the
             right spirit,
joyously, expectantly,
with absolute faith that only the very best is for you?
Over and over again I have told you that I want
only the very best for you.
Why can you not accept this
and cease accepting the second best?

I tell you any old thing will not do.
If you choose to think in that half-hearted way
you will draw any old thing to you,
but this is not My will for you.
I want you to have all the very best in life
and when you have learned
to put first things first in your life,
all the very best will be yours
because I know that you will use it
for the good of the whole
and to My glory.

I do not want you to go through life
with a heavy weight on your shoulders,
bowed down by the cares of the world.
I need you free so that I can work in and through you.
Stop being a worrier;
cast all your cares and burdens upon Me
for you help no one by worrying.

Where is your faith and belief?
Where does your security lie?
You must get your values straight.
What is the use of spending hours in meditation
if you go through life over-burdened?
You must find the perfect balance in life,
be able to raise your consciousness to great heights,
then be able to bring it down into your everyday living.
Live a Life.

The kingdom of heaven is within you.
It is right there waiting for you to recognise it.
You must know this,
believe it,
then bring it about.
The kingdom of heaven is a state of mind
and it is for everyone to seek and find.

Every soul has to long for this before they can find it.
The desire must be there,
and the desire must be so strong
that nothing will be allowed to stand in the way.
You can bring about anything you really desire.
See that your every desire is of the very highest,
that it will benefit the whole
and not just your little self.
Let your mind be stayed on Me,
then your desires will be pure and selfless.

Learn to discipline and control your thinking.
This is something to be achieved in life
though you may have great difficulty
in doing it to begin with.
Never give up,
be patient,
persevere;
and in the end you will be able to control and discipline

your every thought, word and deed
and bring about the most wonderful results in your life.
You will behold miracle upon miracle
because you are working with My laws,
not against them.

The secret of making something work in your life is
first of all, the deep desire to make it work;
then the faith and belief that it can work;
then to hold that clear, definite vision in your
                    consciousness
and see it working out step by step,
without one thought of doubt or disbelief.
Your positive attitude is vitally important
to anything you undertake in life.
When you are determined to do something
wholeheartedly,
perfectly,
and to do it with love
the results are bound to be wonderful.

Start right now to do everything that has to be done
with that right attitude
and see what happens;
when you see everything working out in true perfection
never fail to give thanks
for gratitude keeps the door wide open
and enables more and more to work out in your life.

It is when you start taking things for granted
that all the joy goes out of life
and the door begins to close.

Then the best thing to do
and do quickly,
is to stop and take time to count your blessings,
realise how mightily blessed you are
and then give thanks.
This works like magic in everyone's life.
Why not try it next time life begins to appear dull,
uninteresting and boring,
and see what a transformation it will make
in every way?

The sooner you realise that life is indeed what you
            make it
the more quickly will you behold the right results
and your whole attitude will take a change for the better.

You must learn to be a real optimist
and expect the very best in everything you undertake.
Know that you can and will do it perfectly,
that there will be nothing slapdash in your work
or in your life.
Simply do it unto Me
and to My glory
and you are bound to do everything with love
and therefore in true perfection.

This also applies to the way you look
and the way you behave.

When you are doing everything for Me,
when your greatest desire is to do My will
because of your love for Me,
you will always want to do everything well;
you will always want to look your best,
give of your best,
and you will never be satisfied with anything less
nor be half-hearted over anything.

It is necessary every now and again to take time
and see where you need to change
and then be willing to do so.
If you happen to have a blind spot
be willing to have that blind spot revealed to you
by someone else
and never resent it
for what is done in love can only be for the very best.
Learn to change
and change quickly
without any pull back,
and know that every change is indeed for the very best.

Why not relax,
let go
and let Me take over;
for the more stress and strain there is in your life
the less you get done.

Why not let yourself flow with nature,
flow with the tide
and do what has to be done
quite simply, naturally and joyously?

Why not enjoy life,
instead of going through it with grim determination,
forcing yourself to do this, that or the other
without any joy or love?

Life is really wonderful
when your attitude towards it is right,

and you are in harmony with it,
and cease resisting everything.

Have I not told you,
when you long for something badly enough
you can bring it about?
But always see that your longing
is for something that will benefit the whole
and cease trying to draw things to the self,
for when your motives are selfish
no good can come out of your longings.

When you undertake something,
whatever it is,
do it wholeheartedly
or not at all.
This is so vitally important.
So many souls do a job
simply because they feel it has to be done
and then wonder why life is so drab and dull.

This is not living;
this is merely existing,
and is not the way I want you to live.
This is not the full and glorious life
that I keep telling you about;
the life that I have promised is your true heritage.
But if you fail to claim your true heritage
you have no one but yourself to blame.

Claim that which is yours,
give eternal thanks for it,
and live and move and have your being in it.

Stop talking about it,
stop hearing about it,
simply accept it.

It is so simple.

Why must you make everything so complicated for
            yourself?
Why must you wear sackcloth and ashes
when all My good and perfect gifts are yours?

How foolish can you be,
how blind and stubborn,
refusing to accept the good and perfect which is yours?

How many go through life doing this,
refusing to open their eyes and hearts,
and therefore failing to see My wonders and glories
all around them?

Why not make today a special day?
Really see the very best in everything,
give thanks for everything,
enjoy everything as it should be enjoyed.

I want you to enjoy life,
so why not do so?
Start off by seeing the beauty of nature all around you,
and you will find that one wonderful thing
will lead to the next,
until your whole life is one of wonderment and joy.

'Be ye transformed by the renewing of your minds.'

The more positive and constructive your thinking
the smoother will be the running of your life.

Never forget:
what you put into your deeper mind
is what will come out of it.
Therefore if you feed the mind
with destructive, discontented,
dissatisfied, inharmonious thoughts
those are the ones that will come out of it,
for that which goes in is bound to come out sooner
              or later.

When you fill yourself with things of the Spirit
and function from the level of the Spirit
that which is of the Spirit
will reveal itself in your life and living.

Raise your consciousness,
keep it raised,
never drag it in the mud;
for the more mud and dirt you collect
the more difficulty you will have in ridding
              yourself of it.

Walk in the light and radiate light.
Fill your heart with love and pour forth love.

Make a habit of dwelling on all the glorious things in life,
of seeing the very best in everyone and everything.
Refuse to dwell on the depressing things
but raise your thinking,
let it soar higher and higher like the tiny lark
and sing your song of praise and thanksgiving
for all the wonderful things which are yours.

The more grateful you are,
the more positive you are,
the higher you will soar.
It is the negative things which drag you down;
and the positive, constructive things
which raise you higher and higher.

Never fail to give thanks for everything,
for every lesson you learn, no matter how difficult it
        may be.
Realise that only the very best is bound to come out of it,
that every difficulty is but a stepping stone along
        the way.

There are important lessons which have to be learned
and the sooner you learn them the better.
Never try to shirk them or get round them
but see them for what they are
and face them fairly and squarely.

Surmount them and do it quickly—
speed is essential in overcoming.
There is so much waiting to be revealed
to those who can overcome.

Never be like a gramophone needle
that is stuck in a groove,
repeating the same old mistakes over and over again.
It is not at all necessary,
it is up to you to do something about it.
Nobody else can do it for you.

When you really want to change you can do it.
When you really want to be different
and live a victorious life,
you simply have to make up your mind
that you are going to do it

and you will do it.
Why not start right now
seeing the best in life
and so enjoy life
as it should be enjoyed.

Do you find a real joy in the work you are doing,
in the life you are living?
Do you find real pride in a job
not only well done but perfectly done?
Do you dislike anything that is done
shoddily or half-heartedly?

Is your heart so much in what you are doing,
are you so conscious of the fact
that you are doing everything for Me
and to My honour and glory
that you cannot be satisfied
with anything that is not 'just so'?
This is as it should be;
you should never be satisfied with a job half done
or done in a half-hearted, begrudging manner.
Do all that has to be done with joy and with love,
and let this include everything you do
from the most mundane job
to those vitally important ones.

See that your attitude is right in everything
          you undertake
so that the right vibrations are put into it.

There are many souls who do not yet realise
the importance of vibrations.
Because they are something
that cannot be seen with the physical eye
they feel they do not really matter.

I tell you they are vitally important;
for a job that is done wholeheartedly and with love
carries with it something really tremendous
and will be felt by anyone who is sensitive
and aware of vibrations.
That is why your attitude to everything you undertake
should be right.

Next time you take on a job you do not feel in
            harmony with
take time to go away by yourself
and get into harmony before you continue.
Do not think about yourself and how you feel
but consider all those
who may come into contact with what you do
and how they are going to feel about it.
As you do this
you will find your negative attitude will change
and you will be able to do it
in a completely different frame of mind.
What is more, you will find yourself enjoying doing it
and it will no longer be a bind and a bore.

Learn to blend in,
to harmonise with all life,
to feel and to know the wonder
of being at one and in tune with everything
you do, say and think.

The more you are aware of your oneness with Me
the more you will be in tune with all life.

You have to get into tune;
it does not just happen,
especially when you have been out of tune.
When a musical instrument is out of tune,
time has to be taken to get it into tune again.
When you are out of tune,
you have to take time to get into tune once again,
so there is nothing in you that jars
and strikes a discordant note.

Relax and know that there is time for everything.

Everyone has an equal amount of time,
but it is how you use it that really matters.
Do you use it to the full,
and enjoy every moment of it,
or do you dissipate time by failing to put
         first things first?
Why not first get your values right
and know without any doubt what you put first?

Cease being a slave to time.
Why not make it your servant instead?
Then it will never rule you but you will rule it.

Accept that you can only do one thing at a time,
do it perfectly,
and then move on to the next.

Never try to look too far ahead
and exhaust yourself doing so.

You can only live one moment at a time.
If you try and plan too far ahead
you may be very disappointed
when things do not work out as you planned.

Many changes can take place
in a very short space of time
and in your planning
you know not what those changes are
and cannot account for them.

It is best to live in the moment fully
and let the future take care of itself
and unfold at the right time.

Every moment is precious,
therefore never squander it
in wrong thinking and wrong actions.
Do what you know has to be done, and do it now,
and do it knowing that only the very best will come
          out of it.

Learn to live by inspiration and intuition,
to work by them;
and see the most amazing things come about.
For when you live by the ways of the spirit
anything can happen at any time.
Therefore expect wonder upon wonder to take place
and never fail to recognise My hand in everything
and give Me eternal thanks.
Why not expect the unexpected
and be surprised at nothing?

You are here to live and demonstrate
the most wonderful and unusual happenings,
because you are living and demonstrating
My divine laws in your lives and living.

Never forget this.
Allow My wonders to unfold in everything
and be afraid of nothing.
Fear can hold you back
and nothing must be allowed to do that.

There is much waiting to be revealed,
and My revelations have to come through channels.
You are all My channels,
so open yourselves up
and allow Me to work in and through you.
Let each one receive their specific part
in the vast jigsaw puzzle
and when it has all been pieced together
you will behold the whole.

All will not be revealed to just the few;
I need all of you ready to receive your piece,
so do not fail Me
but offer yourselves to Me so that I can use you.

Never try to hold up progress.
Never try to hold up nature.
When you walk through the garden
and see the beauty and glory of the spring flowers,
never waste time longing for them to remain there
          forever
so that you can always enjoy them.

There is a time and season for everything.
Let go;

let things change around you
without trying to cling to them,
for when the crocus time is over,
it is time for something else just as glorious
to come forth.

Behold the wonder of nature
and give eternal thanks for it.
In nature you see Me:
in the growth of a tree,
in the colour of a flower,
in the scent of a rose,
I am there in everything. Be ever aware of this.
In the beauty and shape of a stone,
in a tiny grain of sand,
in the majesty of the mountains,
I am there.

Flow with the rhythm of nature.
Blend with all there is around you.

See the very best in everything
and you will find yourself surrounded by the best,
for you will draw it all to you like steel to a magnet.
Good attracts good,
just as evil attracts evil.
Fill your life with goodness,
with truth, with love, with understanding
so there is no room for anything of the opposite
        to enter—
and start doing it *now.*

I tell you:
never put off until tomorrow what you can do today.
There is no better time than the ever-present, glorious
        now
to do what you know has to be done.

Never be afraid to face life.
Never be afraid to make mistakes,
as long as you learn by them and are determined
never to make the same mistakes again.

Find out where you are going
and then go ahead
and get there come what may.
Never allow obstacles to stop you from getting there.
When you are really determined to do something
you will always find a way.

Be very clear and definite in all things.
You will never accomplish anything
if you are vague and indecisive.

When you feel uncertain what step you should take next,
do not rush ahead
but take time to be still
and wait and wait if it is necessary
until it has been made very clear to you by Me
what your next step is.
Then go ahead
and do what has to be done without hesitation.

Never fritter away time daydreaming.
It will get you nowhere.
There is a perfect pattern and plan running through
          your life
if you will only take time to be still
and find out what it is.
Let the light of truth illumine the way for you,
so that you do not get lost or misled.

Let Me guide and direct your every step.
Put your whole faith and trust in Me.

How strong is your faith?
How unshakable?

'According to your faith be it unto you.'

When it is really strong enough anything is possible,
absolutely anything.

Faith is not just something to be talked about;
it has to be lived
it has to be demonstrated in your life,
'for faith without works is dead'.

What does it really mean to you to live by faith?
Where is your security?
Is it in people?
In your bank account?
Or is it firmly rooted and grounded in Me?
Take time to ponder on this
and you will know without a shadow of doubt
exactly where your faith and security lie.

Can you joyously and fearlessly take a big step in
            your life,
without any seeming outer security?
When you know something is right,
can you do it without any hesitation?
Can you confidently put your hand in Mine
and say 'Thy will be done,'
and really mean it with your whole heart and soul,
and take that step into the unknown

willing to accept whatever comes?

The only way to build up faith is by first of all
taking those small and even faltering steps
and then bigger ones
until your faith is so strong
that you can take great leaps into the unknown
without any concern,
because you know I am with you always,
you know I am guiding and directing you
and above all you put Me first in everything
and know that I never fail you.

Why not start to live by these laws now?
Why not cease thinking about it
and talking about it
and really live it?

Prove that it does work,
so that all may see and recognise
My hand in your life
and the way you live.
Do everything to My honour and glory
and give eternal thanks.

You cannot live by bread alone
but by My word,
by My promises
which never fail when I am put first
and your faith and trust is in Me—
in the ways of the spirit
and not in human ways.

You cannot build up faith without doing something
        about it.
You cannot live on someone else's faith.
This is something each individual has to develop within.

You cannot reach the top of a mountain
by standing at the bottom and looking up at it.
You have to do the climbing,
you have to want to reach the summit.
The deep desire must be there within
to enable you to get into action.

So it is with faith.
You have to do something about developing it,
you have to put it to the test.
If you have a fall,
you must be willing to pick yourself up
and go on and on
knowing that you will get there in the end,
come what may.

That is faith.

Lift up your hearts and give thanks for everything.
Give thanks for one another,
for the community,
for all you are learning,
for being together and blending together as one big
            family.

Give thanks for the love and understanding
that flows between you,
for being of like mind,
for the knowledge that you are heading
all for the same goal,
even if you are following different paths.

Give thanks for unity in diversity,
for the love that flows between you constantly
and know that love can surmount all difficulties,
all misunderstandings
and draw you together.

Give thanks for life,
for the very breath you breathe,
for every action you take.

Be afraid of nothing.
When love is flowing between you
there can be no fear,
for 'perfect love casts out all fear'.
Where there is love there is perfect understanding.
Therefore love one another.

I can tell you to love one another
but you have to do it.
You can love
when you reach out to one another
and try to understand what makes each tick.
Try to fathom out one another's motives,
not critically or analytically
but because you are genuinely interested in one another
and long to help in every way possible.

Love breaks down all barriers
and maintains an even flow of love between you all
without any ups and downs, likes and dislikes.

Love should never be turned on and off like a tap.
When you love,
love wholeheartedly
and never be afraid to show your love.
You cannot hide love;
it is there for all to see and all to share in.

Let your love be like an open book that all can read.
Why be shy or ashamed of love?
It is the most wonderful thing in the world,
so let that divine love within you flow freely.

Love draws forth love.
Love is not blind,
but it sees the very best in the loved one
and so draws forth the very best.

Never pick and choose whom you are going to love.
Simply keep your heart open
and keep the love flowing to all alike.
That is loving with My divine love;
it is like the sun and shines on all alike.

Love is never exclusive, never possessive,
for when you have found
something truly wonderful and exciting
you long to share it,
not hide it away
or cling on to it for yourself.

So it is with love.
Hold on to it,
and you will lose it.
Let go of it, share it,
and it returns to you a thousandfold
and becomes a joy and a blessing to all who share in it.

Open your hearts to one another,
share your love and appreciation,
and start doing it *now*.

To love one another
you must try to understand one another,
and to understand you have to be able to communicate.
Whether that communication is done in words
or in silent action
matters not
as long as it is done in love,
your heart is open
and the love flows freely.

You have to be very loving
and very tolerant towards your fellows.

When something is clear as crystal to you
it does not mean that it is so with all;
therefore very lovingly
and with the greatest patience and understanding
you must try to convey to others
what you are experiencing
and share those deep, deep feelings within you.
It may not be easy to do this,
but you have to make the effort
because when you really love
you want to share all with those you love.

Love is the answer to all relationships.
Without love there can be no communication.

When there is love
no words need be spoken
for the language of love needs no words;

42

Please write here your name and
address (please PRINT):

Findhorn Press
The Press Building
The Park
Findhorn
Forres IV36 0TZ
Scotland

FINDHORN
Press

Tel +44 (0)1309 690582
Fax +44 (0)1309 690036
e-mail thierry@findhorn.org

Thank you for choosing this book. We appreciate your interest and support.

If you would like to receive our full catalogue of books and other inspirational material, please fill in this card and mail it to us.

☐   Please send book and music catalogue

☐   Please send information about the Findhorn Foundation

In which book did you find this card? _____

Where did you buy this book? _____

Do you have any special interests? _____

there is complete understanding
without a word being spoken.

Where there is love
there are no language barriers
for love can be conveyed in action,
in a silent look,
in the smallest deed,
for love is so great it can be felt and sensed
and you long for the very best for those you truly love.
When you truly love one
you can love all.

So many souls go through life
and never know really the meaning of love.
How blessed you are
who know love
and who are loved.

Love is the key that opens all doors.
Love breaks down all barriers.

Is it any wonder I keep telling you to open your hearts
and love one another.
Only when you have learned to love one another
can you hope to go out into the world
and help those in desperate need.
Compassion towards your fellows is not enough;
there must be love, love, and more love.

For where there is love,
there am I
for I am love;
and you are consciously aware of Me
and of My presence.

You cannot make yourself love anyone;

but when you raise your consciousness
you are able to reach that state
when you know that all is of Me
and there is nothing else,
no separation;
that every soul is of Me,
made in My image and likeness.

Therefore you are one;
and as long as you remain
in that raised state of consciousness
you know the meaning of divine love,
and perfect peace and understanding
fills your whole being.

Be of good cheer;
the time will come when you will be able
to remain in that state of consciousness.
Now you have but fleeting glimpses of what it is like.
Be grateful that you know what it is like
for now you will never rest content
until you have reached that aim
and remain in it for all time.
It needs a dedicated life,
a life fully surrendered to Me and to My work,
a soul who is willing to do My will
no matter what the cost
and to do it with joy and a grateful heart.

Are you willing to live in this way?

44

Let joy and happiness fill your heart.
Realise how mightily blessed you are
and give constant thanks
for those many blessings which are yours.

How can you be downhearted or discontented
when your thoughts are joyous and uplifted,
when your heart is singing songs of praise and gratitude
for these wonderful times that you are living in
and for this wonderful life which is yours?

All that you have to do is to claim it
and enjoy it to the full.

Think of the simplicity of that:
you do not have to strive for it,
fight for it,
hanker after it.
It is yours,
wholly yours
when you claim it
and make it your own.

You do not have to waste time thinking about it
or wondering if you are worthy of it;
it is yours, yours, yours,
when you are ready to accept it.

You can find true happiness and contentment
wherever you are,
whoever you are with,
no matter what you are doing;
for true happiness stems from deep within,
therefore your outer conditions should never rob you
of your inner happiness
which no one and nothing can disturb.

When you have found that inner happiness
and contentment
you will find that you no longer want to live unto
          yourself
but will want to share it
with all those with whom you are in contact;
and the more you share it
the more wonderful it will become.

Happiness cannot be suppressed;
it cannot be hidden away.
It is something that bursts into bloom
like a glorious flower in the rays of the sun,
so that all can see it
and share in its beauty.

It does not matter how dark the night may be;
always remember that joy comes in the morning
as the light breaks through
and the sun rises once again
revealing itself in its full glory and majesty.

Give constant thanks for the new day—
a perfect, unblemished day—
and go forth expecting the very best
to happen during the day.
Know that I go before you to prepare the way;
so just keep consciously aware of Me
and of My divine presence
throughout the day
and watch it unfold in true perfection.

Cease trying to work everything out with your mind,
it will get you nowhere.
Live by intuition and inspiration
and let your whole life be a revelation.
When you live this way

more and more of the new will be revealed to you,
for the new does not come through the mind
but by inspiration
and through the intuition.

That is why it is not necessary to be intellectually clever
to live an inspired spiritual life.

Open your heart
and accept all My good and perfect gifts.
They are there waiting for each one of you
but many of you fail to open your hearts
and stretch forth your hands to accept your rightful
          heritage.
You are either afraid to do so
or feel you are unworthy
or simply do not believe that it is there
and therefore you reject what is waiting for you to claim.

When you have money in the bank
but refuse to accept that it is there
and refuse to draw from that supply
because of your disbelief,
you are the one that suffers lack and has to do without.

My storehouses are full to overflowing
and all that I have is yours;
but you have to do something about it,
you have to claim what is yours.

I can give you one vision after another;

but if you are not faithful
and fail to hold that vision firmly in your consciousness
you will lose it
and it will never manifest in form.
Without vision the people perish.
Without faith and belief
the things of the spirit mean nothing to you.
You cannot live this spiritual life
without faith and belief;
you cannot expect the very best from life
unless you believe that it is yours and claim it.

The new heaven and new earth are here.
Love, peace, harmony, unity are here;
but what are you doing about it?
Are you helping to create it
by your way of life,
by raising your consciousness,
by finding peace and harmony within?
Or are you simply part of the chaos and confusion?
Are you adding your negative, destructive thoughts
to all those around you in the world?

Wake up, watch your thoughts
and see that they are
as positive, loving and constructive
as they can possibly be.

Start right now expecting the very best in life.
Look for the good all around you,
in the people you contact,
in every situation you find yourself in.
Really know and understand
that good comes out of everything
for those who truly love Me
and put Me first in everything.

48

Watch it come about,
and never, never fail to give thanks.

Live this life
daily, hourly, minute by minute.
It is not a life to be lived just one day a week
or only when you feel like it.
It is for truly dedicated souls
who are willing to give all to receive all.

CHANGE

I was shown a pail full of rather ordinary, dull-looking pebbles, of all different shapes and sizes.

Then I saw them poured into a huge tumbler machine and there they were left to tumble for a long time having all their rough edges smoothed until finally they emerged completely transformed into shining and smooth pebbles of real beauty.

I heard the words: 'Only when you have been tried and tested and found not wanting will you emerge transformed as a new age human in your full power and glory.'

Behold, this day I make all things new.
Leave yesterday behind and move swiftly
into this wonderful new day,
knowing that it holds within it
only the very best for each one of you,
and expect only the very best to come out of it.

See My wondrous promises come about one by one;
see My hand in all that is taking place;
behold the birth of the new heaven and new earth.
Dance and sing with joy and give eternal thanks
as you see it emerge
and become substance and form
and grow and develop.

Once it has been born
it cannot go back into its unborn state
but will evolve in true perfection.
You are all part of the new heaven and new earth,
so why not accept your true heritage now
and be grateful that the scales have fallen from your eyes
and you can behold the wonder of it all.

'Fear not, little flock, it is My good pleasure
to give you the kingdom,'
not tomorrow
or some time
but this day.

Can you accept that anything can happen this day
and keep on your toes and be constantly alert?

Are you ready and prepared for the most wonderful
things to take place?
Are you an optimist?
Are you super-positive?

All this helps to hasten things up
and enables you to see
only the very best come out of every situation.
Because you are looking for the very best
you help to bring it about.
You know that all things are possible
and simply refuse to take 'no' for an answer.
By this very positive action
you create the right conditions,
the right environment
for the unfolding of the new.

You become like the midwife,
ready to assist in every way to bring it forth.
It cannot be forced,
it has to unfold step by step.

What does this all mean?
No one knows.
That is why I keep telling you
to be prepared for anything:
new ways
new ideas
a new life.
What you have done in the past will be as nothing
to what you will do in the days ahead.

Your life will be filled with the most wonderful
and unexpected happenings.

Change will be necessary,
therefore do not resist change.

Expansion will be necessary,
therefore do not resist expansion.
Open yourself up and allow yourself to grow
and expand and change
without any effort or resistance.
Just flow into the new
swiftly and smoothly
in perfect unity and oneness.

Those who cannot change because they do not
                want to change
will simply be left behind.
You do not want to be left behind, do you,
after all the wonderful promises I have made to you?

Have no fear of moving into the unknown.
Simply step out fearlessly
knowing that I am with you,
therefore no harm can befall you;
all is very, very well.
Do this in complete faith and confidence.

Can you accept all I am saying to you without any
                doubts or fears?
Can you let go and relax and enjoy all that is
                taking place?

The way to move into the new is with real joy and
                thanksgiving.

Leave yesterday behind.
Waste no more time dwelling on the faults and failures
which dogged your steps and marred the day.
They are finished and done with.

Give thanks for a new day,
for a day unmarred by anything.
It is pure and glorious now,
and it is up to you to keep it so
to advance steadily into it
in absolute confidence and faith
that it is going to be a wonderful day.

Everything is going to fall into place perfectly;
everything is going to run smoothly;
everyone you meet will be a joy and delight to talk to;
not one negative or unpleasant thought or idea
will enter your consciousness.

In the newness of the day all is very, very well.
All is perfect.
You are going to keep it so
with My constant help and guidance
by being consciously aware of Me
and of My divine presence,
by calling upon Me
and waiting upon Me in quietness and confidence.

When you feel that you have reached the end
and that you cannot go one step further,
when life seems to be drained of all purpose:
what a wonderful opportunity to start all over again,
to turn over a new page.

This is something everyone can do
if they really want to,
if they can swallow their pride

and accept in true humility
that of themselves they are nothing;
that they only make a mess of their lives
when they try to handle them on their own;
if they are willing to hand their lives over to Me,
to let Me run them;
to realise that when I am in control
all things are possible.

Give constant thanks for this new day
for a new way
for a new opportunity to start again.

There is no need to remain in the 'Slough of Despond'
if you do not want to.
You can be lifted to great heights.
You can walk in the glorious light
with your heart filled with love
when you choose to do so.
You must do the choosing,
you have to make the decision to change.

What are you going to do about it?

Realise that I have need of you
and when you are in a negative state
you shut yourself off from Me.
It is up to you to choose of your own free will
to contact Me again,
for, remember—I never enter where I am not invited.

Call upon Me—and I will answer you.
I will be with you in trouble.
I will uplift you,
I will set your feet upon the right path,
I will guide your every step.
I will never fail you or forsake you.

I am with you always.

Life is full and overflowing with the new.
But it is necessary to empty out the old
to make room for the new to enter.
The emptying out process can be very painful,
but it is very necessary
for when you have been emptied of the old,
you may experience that feeling of barrenness,
of having nothing to hold on to,
of being alone and bereft of everything.
You may even feel that I have forsaken you,
that life is completely dead and empty
with no meaning to it,
and you want to throw up your hands in despair
and run away from everything.

Try to realise that if you are going through a time
        like this
it is this process of being emptied of the old
so that you can be refilled with the new.
Never give up hope
but hold on
until you can start again
in newness of spirit and in truth.
You can become as a little child
and enjoy to the full the wonderment of this new life
as you gradually become infilled by it.

You have to be willing to unlearn so much
to make room for all those new and wonderful truths
        to enter
and become part of you.

58

It is more difficult to unlearn than it is to learn,
for many souls cling on to what they know
because they are afraid of losing their feeling of security
their feeling of superiority
and are uneasy at the idea of being born again
in spirit and in truth
to enable them to enter the new.
They cannot bear to be parted from all the knowledge
they have acquired in this life,
and many refuse to start again,
which results in the parting of the ways.

No one can enter the new without a real change of heart;
and you can experience a real change of heart
only when you choose to do so of your own free will.
No one can make you change,
they can only show you the way.
You have to take it.
You have to start the wheels turning and keep
            them turning.

Every day is a new day,
therefore expect something new and different each day;
never be satisfied to drift along in the same old way
day after day.
Start each day by getting in touch with Me
and then expect the most wonderful things
            to come about.

How can life be dull and mundane
when you are in tune with the source of all life?

Expect wonder upon wonder to take place.
Be prepared for anything to happen at any time.
Behold the new unfold in true perfection,
and give eternal thanks for everything.

Every day you can learn something new and wonderful,
but what you do with that lesson is up to you:
you can live it
and put it into practice
and see how wonderfully it works;
or you can tuck it away into the subconscious
and draw it out at a later date,
but sooner or later you will have to live it—
if not in this life, in the next.

The sooner you put it into practice the better
because with practice comes change:
change of heart,
change of outlook,
change of attitude
change of a whole way of life.
You can be transformed as you learn
to live and demonstrate that lesson,
whatever it may be.

Unless you allow a very small child to do things
        for itself:
to feed itself,
to walk, to dress itself,
to write, to draw,
to express itself,
it will never develop and become independent
and be able to stand on its own feet
and make its own decisions.

You have to stand back

and allow it to make mistakes,
to take a long time to master what it is learning to do.
You have to be very patient
and wait
and watch
no matter how tempted you are to rush forward
and do it for the child to save time.

How often do I have to stand back
and very lovingly watch you fumbling
and struggling with life
so that you can learn a vitally important lesson from it—
a lesson never to be forgotten
once it has been mastered.
I have infinite love and patience.

If only you would open your eyes,
you would realise that life is a classroom in a school,
you are learning all the time;
you are absorbing the most wonderful truths
which will become part of you;
you will find yourself living and demonstrating them.

It may take time for this to come about,
but sooner or later it will;
it is up to you how soon.
You can learn quickly if you choose,
or you can go off and experiment on your own
and try out your own methods
which may take you far longer.

What you do and how you do it
is up to you.
I am there to show you the way,
but you have to take it.
No one else can take it for you,
no one else can live your life for you.

What are you doing with your life?
Are you content to drift through it
doing what you want to,
living the way you want to live,
without a thought for anyone else?
You are free to do this.
Many, many souls live this way
and then wonder why they are so unhappy
and discontented.

It is only when you learn to forget the self
and live for others
that you will find real peace of heart
and true contentment.

Learn to give and not just take all the time.
Why not give on one level and receive on another?
Life is a two-way thing,
a constant giving and receiving.
I keep on telling you that you cannot live unto yourself
and find real happiness and satisfaction in life.

Live for the whole
and give to the whole,
and be whole.

Rejoice
and give eternal thanks
for you know that you live forever
and you do it one day at a time,
living each moment fully and gloriously,
forgetting the past
with no concern for the future;
simply accepting that life has no beginning and no end,
that life is eternal
and you are hope eternal.

I am life
and I am within you.
I live and move and have My being in you.
I am infinite.

You are one with Me,
you are one with all life.

All the time you are growing
and expanding in consciousness,
you are beginning to understand the mystery
        and wonder
of life eternal and your realisation of oneness with Me,
the creator of life,
the creator of all.

Step by step
you move onward and upward
filled with peace, tranquillity and serenity
realising that as all is in My hands
therefore you have nothing to concern yourselves with.

Become as little children,
free and joyous,
and life will be a continual source of delight for you,
a veritable wonderland

with something new and exciting round every corner.

Believe in life
and live it fully.
It is when you try to look too far ahead into the future
that life becomes a real burden,
and to many brings fear,
uncertainty,
even lack of faith and belief.

Unless you believe that life is eternal
and that you are immortal,
life has little or no meaning for you.
Your attitude is that you are here today
and gone tomorrow
so you might as well grab all you can out of life
whilst you can.

Change this attitude:
realise that life is eternal,
you have much to give as well as receive,
life is a two-way thing
and as you learn to give, so you will receive.
Life becomes very empty
and unfulfilled
when you keep taking and give nothing.

When you breathe the breath of life, you breathe it in;
but you cannot retain it for any length of time
without breathing it out.
This is also a two-way thing,
a giving
and receiving,
for without it there would be no life.

Open your heart
and give all you can

of the gifts which have been given you.
Give of your love,
your wisdom,
your understanding;
give of the intangible
as well as the tangible things which are yours;
give and give and go on giving
without any thought of self,
without any thought of cost
or what you will get out of it.

Your giving must be wholehearted and joyous,
then you will find the very act of giving
will bring with it joy and happiness untold.

Let me remind you again:
that you all have something to give,
so find out what you have to give
and then give it.
Never forget there are many levels on which you
        can give.
What level can you give on?
Do not just give what is easy to give,
but give where it really hurts
and grow and expand as you do so,
for only the very best can come out of your giving.

65

I have given you the right way to live,
and as you follow My laws
and obey them
your life becomes rich and mightily blessed.
Disobey those laws
and sooner or later
you will find yourself slipping downhill.
Things may go smoothly for a while,
you may appear to prosper as you go your own way
and do what you please
but the time will come when things will catch up on you
and down and down
you will go,
until you realise where you have gone wrong
and are determined to do something about it.

This is when you have to start putting first things first;
when you have to turn away
from your waywardness
to seek Me and My kingdom first.
This is not an easy thing to do
when you have reached rock bottom
and feel there is no purpose in life;
yet this is what you will have to do.

Put your feet on the bottom rung of the ladder
and start climbing
no matter how difficult it may be at the time;
as you pull yourself up to the next rung
and gradually work your way
out of the darkness and despair you have sunk into,
life begins to change for you
and you will find a real purpose in your life and living.

Where are you on that ladder of life?
Have you reached rock bottom
and begun the upward climb?

Have you been willing to give up everything in your life
to put Me first,
not because you are afraid
but because of your deep love for Me
and your longing to do My will and walk in My ways?
Can you say, 'Let Thy will be done'
and really mean it
and be willing to do
whatever I ask you to do
no matter how strange or foolish it may appear
in the eyes of others?
This takes courage
and such a deep inner knowing and certainty
that nothing will be able to throw you off balance.

Only those who are strong
will be able to follow this spiritual path
and reach the goal.
I keep telling you this life is not for weaklings.
It is not for those who fail to put Me first;
it is not for those who choose to go their own way
and refuse to listen to Me and to My word.

There are no short cuts in this spiritual life.
You have to seek and find your own salvation;
no one else can do it for you.

That is why I keep on telling you over and over again
that you have to stand on your own feet
and do your own seeking,
your own thinking.
In fact you have to do your own spiritual work,
you cannot expect anyone else to do it for you.

Surely you see this clearly by now,
so why not get on
and do something about it *now*.

In your spiritual growth never strain;
stretch, yes—but strain, no.

Stretching is a gradual process.
If you have ever watched a cat stretch
you will understand:
every ounce and every inch of it gradually stretches
until it has stretched itself
from the tip of its nose
to the tip of its tail;
and when it has done that
it is perfectly relaxed;
there is absolutely no strain whatsoever.

That is the way I want you to be able to stretch,
gradually, gradually
until the whole of you has grown in the process
and yet is perfectly relaxed.
As you keep on doing it
you will understand what I mean.

When there is strain
there is a dividing up;
but when there is just a gradual stretching
there is a complete oneness.
It is a unifying process
and stretching should be gradual.

So often you do it in jerks
and then wonder why you suffer from aches and pains;
whereas if you stretched that little bit more each day,

stretching up and up,
you would have no aches and pains
but a real joy and delight in so doing
and a feeling of growth.

A plant does not grow in fits and starts,
it grows gradually.
You are unaware of its actual growth
but see it change and develop.

Your spiritual growth should be the same,
and if it is not, do something about it.
I do not want you up in the heights one moment
and down in the depths the next;
this is far too great a strain on all your faculties,
that is the way you can so easily become unbalanced.
I need you perfectly balanced,
like a precision instrument.
Therefore do whatever has to be done
steadily and with precision.

This will call for a real control of yourself
which will not be easy,
but it is so very important
and with My help you can and will do it.

There is much to be done,
but there is time for everything.
Live fully in the moment
and live a full and joyful life.
Great things will be accomplished in this way.

Know that all is very well;
be very still
and absorb the wonder of My presence.
I am with you always,
be ever conscious of Me.

Be very, very still
and allow every new experience
to take place in your life without any resistance
          whatsoever.
You do not have to do anything,
you simply have to *be*
and let things happen.
It is so important that you stop trying,
that you stop making an effort
and let go completely
to let Me work in and through you
My wonders to perform.

Every deep experience you have must be recorded.
I tell you to hide nothing.
You have nothing to be ashamed of,
you are mightily blessed.

All the time you are receiving confirmation
that these deep inner experiences you are having
are not just your imagination,
that they are not simply illusion
but reality
and become more and more real to you each day.

There are times when you feel you are living
in an entirely new world;
and this is when you start worrying
and wondering if it is a world of illusion.
Be at peace and rest assured,
this is indeed the world of reality.

You are simply being raised into higher dimensions
and are viewing everything
from that raised state of consciousness
and there is absolutely nothing to be concerned about.

Look upon all this
as if you have come to live in a new country;
you have a new language to learn,
new ways of living
your eating and sleeping habits all have to be changed,
your whole environment is different.

Do not try to take any of your old life with you,
cut away completely from the old,
leave it all behind;
you simply have no room for the old
in this new life you are now living.

Never waste time looking back
to see what you have left behind.
The future is so truly glorious
that you will have no need
to hanker for anything of the old
which you have left behind you.
That is all finished and gone.
Let it fade into nothingness;
as you do so you will find a new joy and freedom,
a new peace and happiness
as you blend into your new environment
and become part of it,
living it to the full and enjoying every moment of it.

You need never feel lost in this new life
for I am there to guide you
and teach you
and instruct you in new ways.
There is much to learn;

but you will learn very quickly
as you leave the old behind and forget it,
replacing it with the new and wonderful.

All this is happening to you now.

Are you alert and receptive to new and fresh ideas?
Are your thoughts positive and constructive at all times?
Do you eliminate all negative, unhappy
and depressing thoughts
and see the very best
in everything that is happening in your life?
Can you see a wonderful pattern and plan
running through all that is happening to you
and know with deep inner knowing
that only the very best will come out of it,
even if it means a complete upheaval in your life?

Start from this moment to watch your thoughts
            and ideas
and do not let them wander aimlessly around.
Be in complete control of them
and select only those thoughts and ideas
which will bring the very best to the whole.

Why dwell on the negative
when the very best,
the positive,
is just around the corner
if you are willing to expand your consciousness
            and find it?

Never be afraid of change,
of the new.
Learn to let go
and move forward in absolute freedom
and once you have let go
never look backward but ever forward.
Once you have set the ball rolling
and have accepted a completely new life,
have no regrets
but accept it all with real joy and thanksgiving.
Regrets can hold you back
and can prevent the most wonderful things
taking place in your life.
Keep open so that anything can happen.

Never be afraid to tread the path alone.
Know which is your path
and follow it wherever it may lead you;
do not feel you have to follow
in someone else's footsteps.
When you take time to be still in the silence
you will know what is your specific path.

It takes strength and courage to follow the path,
especially when you have to go alone.
You must not just follow the crowd
because it is easier and more comfortable.
Find out what My will is for you
and follow it wherever it may take you.

Turn within more and more,
attune your consciousness to the very highest,
and watch My plan unfold for you step by step.

Those steps may come thick and fast.
Let them come.
When I tell you that My glorious plan

73

will unfold step by step
you visualise it all happening slowly.
Nothing will happen slowly now.
Everything is being speeded up.

Nevertheless it will be an unfoldment
because all will come about in perfect timing.
Just let it come and do not try
to stop anything taking place
because you are afraid of the speed at which it is coming.

My timing is always perfect.
You know this,
so why not accept it
and go along with it?
Let there be no resistance in you
but find perfect freedom and joy as the plan unfolds.
It is a truly wonderful plan
and you are all part of it.
You each have your own part to play in it,
that is why it is so important for you each to find
what your part is
and for you to do this now.

Do not drift through another day without finding it out.

Still your stress and striving.
Be at peace and let Me take over.

When you can really let go
and let Me do the work

74

you will accomplish wonder upon wonder;
for nothing of the self will stand in the way
to hold anything up
and therefore anything can happen.

The higher your aims and goals the better.
Never limit yourself in any way,
simply know that you can accomplish
anything that you set out to do
because you are drawing your help and strength
            from Me
and there is no such thing as defeat or failure.
Whatever has My hallmark on it is bound to succeed
and only the highest results can come from it.
Therefore keep your consciousness raised,
get into tune with all life,
and behold the most wonderful results.

You cannot expect these results
unless you are in rhythm
with the highest good within you
and can flow freely with all that is going on
and move through all that would hold you up.
There are many things in life
that would hold you up from reaching your goal.
Sweep them all aside
and refuse even to contemplate failure for one second.
Simply know you can and you will succeed
and success will be yours in everything you undertake.

Work with My laws,
not against them.
When you work against them
you are fighting a losing battle
and will get nowhere.

When there is tension in you

seek within
and find out what you are fighting against
to cause that tension.
You may be sure there is something there
holding up your progress
and preventing you from reaching your highest good.

Let your only desire be to do My will
and walk in My ways, come what may,
and allow nothing to stand in the way
to prevent this from taking place.

Never try to make excuses for yourself;
you ought to know better than to do that by now.

When you take time to seek
you will know what My will is for you
and then it is up to you to obey it without hesitation.
When you are working and living in harmony
you will know the meaning of true freedom—
freedom of heart, mind and spirit;
the sort of freedom that enables you to rise
to the greatest heights
and plumb the deepest depths
and find perfect balance in everything.

When you are able to do this
you will find untold wisdom
and understanding flowing from you,
and in this state of consciousness
I can use you to help bring down
the new heaven and new earth.

I cannot do this
as long as there is conflict and stress within you
for they block the flow.
I need you free

and true freedom stems from within,
with perfect peace of heart and mind;
and this you will find only when you are in tune
        with Me.

So again I say to you:
get into tune
and do it now.

Take time to be still
and listen to all the wonderful sounds around you.
Enjoy them to the full
and give constant thanks
that you have ears to hear with.

How many times during the day do you stop
and listen to those many inner and outer sounds?
Do you ever stand still listening
and counting how many different sounds you can hear?
This will make you more sensitive,
more alert,
more aware.

When you have tried that
and become more and more aware
of life everywhere around you,
why not try listening to those inner intangible sounds
which can only be heard in absolute stillness and silence;
that stillness which passes understanding
when you become in tune with the things of the spirit,
with the things that really matter in life?

In that state of perfect peace and stillness
your whole life changes,
a deep tranquillity and serenity
are radiated from within.
In that state there can be no harsh or jarring sounds
because you become one with the whole of life
and blend perfectly with that whole.
You feel uplifted, inspired,
filled with illumination,
for your whole being is filled
with My divine light
and you can see all things clearly.
You understand not with the mind
but with the higher consciousness
and with the heart.

You are in love with all life
and that includes all your fellow humans.
You do not know the meaning of hate,
jealousy, envy;
but you know what it means to love your enemies,
for you find that you no longer have any enemies
because your heart has expanded so much
that you know what it is like to love with
          My divine love.

The self is completely forgotten
and your life is one of love and service
to your fellows,
of giving, giving, giving.

What joy this brings,
unbelievable joy.
It is only when you are giving
that you find that wonderful inner joy and happiness,
which nothing and no one can take from you
and which nothing can dampen.

Joy comes with service
and service comes with dedication.
Dedicate yourself to Me and to My service now
and feel yourself expand as you do so.
Feel your consciousness raised to that state
where you know the meaning of oneness with all
           creation,
your oneness with Me.

At first this state of consciousness
may only last a very short time,
but as you climb the ladder,
each rung takes you nearer and nearer to the goal—
your conscious awareness of Me,
Keep on climbing and never give up.

To live in peace and harmony
with yourself
and with your fellows
you must learn to live by My laws
and to demonstrate them
in your daily life and living.

When you are in tune with life
you are in rhythm with My divine laws,
everything runs smoothly,
life flows with ease and grace
and there is nothing jarring or inharmonious.

Is your life running smoothly?
Are you content with what you are doing?

Do you feel at peace with the world?
Or is your life full of ups and downs?
Are you dissatisfied with the way you are living?
With the work you are doing?
Do you find it difficult to blend and harmonise
with those around you?
Do you blame your discontent and dissatisfaction
on those with whom you are in contact
and on your circumstances and situation?
Do you feel that if you were somewhere else
all would be well and you would be at peace?

When you are at perfect peace deep within
it does not matter where you are
or who you are with
or what very ordinary, mundane job you are doing.
Nothing will be able to disturb you
or throw you off balance
because you are perfectly balanced
and in harmony within.

Instead of fighting against your circumstances
you learn to flow with them
and so find that inner peace and understanding
deep within.

Why not look within when things are not
          going smoothly
and see where you are out of tune;
never try to blame anyone else
for the negative state you are in.

Stop looking for a scapegoat in your life
but be willing to face the truth within yourself
and right your own wrongs.

When you realise that you have only yourself to blame

when things become difficult
and you get out of tune,
you will also realise that you are the one
to do something about rectifying those wrongs,
that you do not have to wait
for someone else to change and do something about it.
You can start right now doing something about it
            yourself.

How many times have you said to yourself lately:
'If only such and such a person would not interfere,
if only such and such a thing had not happened,
how different everything would be.'

Why not stop pointing your finger at someone else?
Stop blaming that someone else
and start righting your wrongs yourself—right now.

Stop trying to run away from yourself;
you can never do it
so you might as well accept it
and start changing yourself
instead of others and your surroundings.

You can go to the ends of the earth
but *you* will always be there.
You are the one to change.
You are the one who can do something about it.

Do not waste any more time thinking
but get into action now,
and see how you can change your whole life
by your right and positive thinking and outlook
and get into tune.

Keep on and on expanding your consciousness.
You find you are beginning to understand
and to live things
that in the past have just been words,
words that have been repeated over and over again,
and you have thought 'What lovely,
          what wonderful words,'
but they were not living words.

You are the one to make My words live,
you have to give them life force,
and this you have failed to do so often in the past;
but now as your consciousness has begun to expand,
you are beginning to put into action all I am saying.

This will make all the difference to your life and
          your living.
It means that by your action you will begin to see
My promises come about,
promises which I have made to you over and over again,
but until you realised you had to do something
to bring them about,
until you realised you had to become My hands and feet,
those promises had to lie dormant.

It makes you want to go back over past messages
and find out where you have missed the way.
That would be a complete waste of time.
All I want you to do is to live to the full now,
studying carefully each day
what I have to say to you

82

and then immediately taking action
when action is needed
no matter what it may be;
and never wasting time questioning and querying
what I have to say.
In this way you really will begin
to see things happen in your life.
There are many big and wonderful changes
which will come about
as small actions are taken to unlock doors.

A word here,
a letter there,
an action somewhere else—
all these are like keys which unlock doors
which have been locked a very long time.
Sometimes you will find the keys are rusty,
or even the locks are rusty;
this is where the soothing oil of love and understanding
needs to be poured on:
sometimes very gently drop by drop,
and other times plenty needs to be applied to lubricate;
great sensitivity is needed all the time.

Each day you should feel
that you have made a step forward and upward
along the path.
Some days that step may be easy,
you may not even notice you have moved ahead;
another day you find that one step forward
has been a real effort,
that the way has been very rough and steep,
and you may feel quite exhausted from the exertion.

Then rest in My peace and stillness;
awaken refreshed,
and renewed,

and determined to take the next step
that needs to be taken,
and advance along the way
knowing that every step which is taken
brings you ever nearer the goal.

Never despair,
never give up,
every effort is well worthwhile,
every obstacle which you manage to surmount
is yet another milestone along the way.

Seek My help at every step;
when I give instructions, act upon them;
I am your guide,
follow thou Me.

Pour your whole being into everything you do
and do whatever it is wholeheartedly
with real joy
and love
and to My honour and glory.
Behold the most wonderful results,
for when everything is done in purest love,
how could it be otherwise?

Flow with the rhythms of nature,
not against them;
nature's rhythms are perfect
and nothing is out of timing,
out of season,

out of place;
there is a place for everything
and everything is in its proper place.
Peace and harmony reign
and My kingdom is come.

I will guide and direct the whole of your life
when you will let Me.
When you are willing to surrender your all to Me
and hold nothing back,
then your every need will be wonderfully met
and your life will flow with abundance.
There will be nothing in you to stop that flow of
          abundance,
for you open the floodgates
when you surrender your all to Me.

Let not fear hold you back.
You have nothing to lose and everything to gain
if you will only realise this
and surrender all into My hands.
Perfect love casts out all fear.
You cannot fear Me and love Me at the same time
for love and fear cannot walk hand in hand.
They are like oil and water and do not mix,
so transform all fear into love
and behold the wonderful way
in which your life will flow
and how everything will fall into place perfectly.

Fear is the biggest hang up in life;
therefore the sooner you are freed of it, the better.
Just to remove fear is not enough,
you must then fill up the vacuum with love and
          more love
until there is so much love in you
that there is no room for anything else.

I can then function in perfect freedom
and My wonders and glories can manifest in form
        in your life
and all will be very, very well.

Take one step at a time to get into rhythm.
Absorb it into your whole being
until it becomes a part of you
and you vibrate with that rhythm of all life
and know the meaning of wholeness,
of being in tune with the whole of creation,
and therefore in tune with Me.

I am the creator of all creation,
I am the wholeness of life.
Raise your consciousness,
expand your consciousness,
realise that I am within each one of you,
that this wholeness is there within you,
that nothing can separate you from the wonder of this
except your own limited consciousness.

Why not let go
and let it expand
and expand
and allow nothing to stop that expansion of
        consciousness
until you can accept that I am in you
and you are in Me
and we are one, one, one.

Do not just toy with the idea,
but really *know* it
and accept it.
You cannot move into the new until you do.

There are far too many of you

who are still toying with the idea of oneness,
of wholeness;
but who are still not quite willing to accept it as fact
and plunge right in in absolute faith and trust
and accept your oneness with Me.

Waste no more time.
Do it now.

Spring is here.
The new age is here.
Awake from your slumbers
and behold the wonder of the times,
for these are truly wonderful times you are all living in.

Wonder upon wonder is waiting to unfold.
See the very best in everything that is taking place.
Expect changes
and go along with them
allowing nothing in you to hold them up.

Never be afraid of the new,
of the unknown,
but step fearlessly into it
knowing that I am with you always
and that I will never leave you or forsake you.
When I am for you, who can be against you?
Recognise Me in everything
and give Me the honour and glory.
Take nothing to the self
that might stop that wonderful flow within.

This is the golden age that you are moving into.

Change and pain come with the birth of anything new.
But once the actual birth has taken place pain is
          forgotten.
So be not concerned
nor struggle against the changes
which are taking place at this time.

The darkest hour comes before the glorious dawn.
The dawn is there.
It comes in perfect rhythm
and nothing can stop it coming about.
The whole universe functions in that perfect rhythm,
so why don't you?
Get into rhythm
and flow with it instead of fighting against it.

The more you fight against change
the more pain and suffering you cause yourself.
It is resistance that causes the pain.
Let go
and let Me take over
and be at perfect peace.

Seek and find peace, serenity and tranquillity
at all times
and let it infil your whole being;
project this state of consciousness all around you,
for that which is within is reflected without.

Let there be no feeling of competition within you.
When you realise that each of you
has your specific part to play in the whole,
all that spirit of competition will disappear,
and you will be able to relax
and be yourself.

How much simpler life becomes
when you cease trying to be something you are not.

Let there be no round pegs in square holes.
You each have your part to play in the whole,
so play it to the very best of your ability.

I tell you to love one another.
Are you really doing this?
Or are you still just tolerating each other,
making excuses for yourselves
by saying that there are certain souls
you cannot be expected to blend with
since you are poles apart
and it would be just like trying to mix oil and water
to ask you to love them?

You are all My beloveds
and the sooner you realise this the better;
for you are all one in My sight
and My love flows to each one of you alike.
When you can accept your oneness with Me
you will be able to accept your oneness with each other,
and learn to live and work as one.

ONENESS

I was shown the rays of a light coming down on to the earth, and they spread over the earth.

Then I was shown rays of light coming up, and as they rose higher and higher they seemed to draw closer together until they blended and became one, one great ray of light going up to the source of all light.

I heard the words: 'Be at peace. Rise up. All is one in My divine light.'

Be at peace
and see a clear pattern and plan
running through all your lives.
Nothing is by chance.

There are times when you are blind
and cannot see that pattern;
in fact you question and query certain happenings
and even become dismayed
because things do not work out
as you imagined they would.

It is best to have no fixed ideas
unless I give those ideas to you
and ask you to hold them in your consciousness
so they can be manifested in form
and brought down on to this level.

Then do it with a will
and never at any time
allow anything to interfere.

My ways are perfect,
though very strange at times.
You even become baffled and bewildered
at the very strangeness.

Remember, My ways are not human ways.
Choose always My ways and walk in them,
looking neither to the left nor to the right,
never allowing yourself to be influenced by anyone.

You desire only to do My will,
therefore do it.
Seek it at all times
and then go ahead unhesitatingly
knowing that all is very, very well.

Many, many souls will be drawn to this place.
Some will come to give
and others to receive.

Some will come strong in faith and belief,
and others weak and unsure,
wondering why they have been drawn here,
wondering what it is all about.

All their needs are to be ministered to.
You each have something unique to give to each soul.
Give and give unstintingly,
let nothing be too much trouble.
It is My work you are doing,
so do it with a full and joyous heart.

Take all who come on your heart;
be fearful of no one.
Love breaks down all barriers,
love surmounts all obstacles,
love unites and brings peace and harmony;
therefore let My divine love flow through you
and out to those in need.

Try not to step back into old routines,
old ruts and habits.
All is new.
Great changes are in process,
nothing can ever be the same again,
ahead is the glorious new.

Look not back,
but ever forward,
in joy and anticipation,
never in apprehension
for all is in My hands.

Keep very close to Me
and only the perfect can come about.
Rejoice and be glad
for these are great and glorious days.

This time you spend with Me each morning
should benefit you for the rest of the day.
You are like a battery being recharged:
by the end of the day you have run low
and need that time for recharging
so you can start the day aright.

If you fall asleep at night in the right state,
having surrendered yourself to Me,
you can be recharging all night.
Then in the morning you receive
your final topping up by Me
by spending this time
in prayer,
in meditation,
in listening to My word
and recording it.

Then in that topped-up state
you start the new day full of zest

and determined to do better than yesterday
and to obey My word in everything.

Every day should carry you a step forward
in this spiritual life.
You may not always see the step that has been taken
or even feel one has been taken,
it may be such a small one;
but as long as you are determined to move ahead
you will do so.

So much lies in your hands,
in your decision.
If you just sit there
and say you can't take another step forward,
you won't.
But if each morning you start off determined to do
          My will
and to follow in My footsteps,
you will surely do so
and advance along the path I have chosen for you,
never holding up the work.

There is really no time for complacency.
There is always room for advancement,
for change,
but it rests in your hands whether you do so.

You cannot be made to do it,
you are free to make your own decision
over everything.
You can be helped or shown a path
but you need not take it.
The very next step you take along the path
must be made by your own effort.

So don't dither on the brink.

There is a great and glorious future ahead,
so move ahead steadily.
Keep on changing,
unfolding like a flower
in the sunshine of My love and guidance.
Let there be no resistance.
Seek My inner peace constantly.

Keep a sense of humour.
The enemy hates it when you can see the funny side
of some of his subtle tricks
and laugh in his face.
This makes him turn his back on you and flee.
So laugh,
try to see the funny side at all times.

Some days the enemy seems to lurk around every corner;
yet by the end of the day
you do not feel weighed down
or dragged down by him
if you are able to laugh at him
and see the funny side at every turn,
in this way defeating him and rising above him.

Keep on rising.
Do not allow yourself to be dragged down by anything.
I am with you always,
simply raise your consciousness
and find Me
and follow Me.

It does not matter how menial the task may be,
you can always do it with Me.
I am with you always.

Never hold Me afar off
and feel that what you are doing you must do alone,
because you could not ask Me to share it with you.
I long for you to share every second of your living
        with Me;
I cannot stress this too strongly.
I do not want you to leave Me out of any part of
        your life,
and this you will find you will be able to do
more and more easily
as you become aware that we are one.

That is the most precious truth;
once accepted fully
and there is a constant awareness of that oneness,
you can no longer live a separate life from Me;
all you do will be with Me,
for Me,
to My honour and glory.

At times you are very much aware of this oneness;
then like a child who wants to go off on its own
        exploring,
you wander away and forget all about Me.
You find life is good,
you enjoy being on your own,
you wonder why you don't do this more often,
everything is going smoothly.

Then without any warning you slip
and find yourself in a bottomless bog.
You are being slowly sucked down by the mud.
You try to get out:

but the more you struggle
the deeper you sink.
You shout for help,
and the more desperate you get
the louder your shouts become.

Then you feel yourself being lifted out of that
            clawing mud
and are lying on firm ground
filthy,
exhausted,
very penitent
and determined not to wander off on your own again.

This you do from time to time;
but those times become less and less
until finally you realise how hopeless life is without Me.

You need Me all the time.
There are far too many pitfalls along the way of life
to try to do it without a guide;
so accept Me as your constant guide and companion
and let us traverse life together.

I will take you to the heights,
and I will take you to the depths,
but no harm will befall you;
you can feel absolutely secure strapped to Me
if you should stumble and fall.

I am there to take the strain
and pull you up again
and set you on your feet.
If you hurt yourself in your fall,
I am there to heal you
and care for you.

This is the wonderful close relationship I long for
with all My children.
I am indeed closer than breathing,
nearer than hands and feet;
but you must be ever aware of this
and never for one instant think otherwise.
This is our true relationship—
lift up your heart in deep, deep gratitude.

I keep on stressing the importance
of this relationship between us,
because it is so vital
and you must become aware of it at all times:
because when there is chaos and confusion all
           around you,
unless you are absolutely sure of your security
you will be unable to stand firm
but will turn and flee
and there will be nowhere to flee to.

Therefore be firmly grounded in Me,
then nothing can touch you or move you.

You will see clearly one day
why I keep repeating Myself
and you will be everlastingly grateful.

Every experience in life,
no matter how painful,
which draws you ever nearer to Me,
and enables you to realise

that you can do nothing without Me,
that you need Me at all times and in all places,
is something to be everlastingly grateful for
and should be accepted with deep gratitude.

You are now learning the true meaning
of being one with Me.
It is one thing to be told this,
to read about it,
to ponder on those words;
but it is an entirely different thing to learn to live them,
and vibrate with them
until they become a part of you.

This was something you experienced recently
for the first time,
a never-to-be-forgotten experience
which you are to learn to put into practice constantly.
This will require a constant stretching
on your part to begin with;
you will have to hold this thought within your mind
and when it fades away
you will have to bring it back consciously.

Yes, it will fade away,
and you will even have doubts about it from time
          to time;
but as you stretch out and reach for the knowledge,
so will you instantly become aware
and once again you will know
without a shadow of doubt
that you are indeed one with Me,
your God, your Beloved.
And as your consciousness is raised,
you will know just how to behave at all times:
act only as I would act,
do only what I would do,

101

say only the things I would say,
live only the life I would live.

You will indeed learn to live this life
of at-one-ment with Me
with real joy in your heart.
You will know the meaning of the peace
which passes all understanding.

I hear the cry from your heart,
'How long? How long?'
It will not be long.
As you stretch forth all the time,
and are never content to drift aimlessly,
you will reach the goal of perfection.

Yes, I did say 'perfection'.
Is that not your goal?
Is that not what you are striving for,
to be like Me,
to be ever at one with Me?

I hear you say, 'How can that be in this world?'
I want you to know:
not only *can* it be in this world
but it *must* be.
Have I not asked you to stretch up
and bring down My kingdom of heaven
here upon this earth
and see that My will is done here on earth
as it is in heaven?

I never ask you to do the impossible.
As you learn to live and move and have your being
        in Me
so you will bring about My will.
But live it,

102

cease talking about it.

Seek Me at every turn
and you will know exactly how I would act;
then follow in My footsteps
and remember always
that My ways are very strange
and My ways are not human ways,
so there is no fixed pattern for you to adhere to.

Act from the spirit,
walking in My ways,
and behold My wonders and My glories.

You have at least reached the stage
when you know that you really need
this time of peace and stillness each morning,
when you can seek and find Me
and we can walk and talk together
without any interruptions.

During the day there are so many things to be done,
there are so many interruptions,
it is not easy to find an outer peace.

Of course you can find that inner peace at all times
and in all places;
but even that becomes virtually impossible
unless you take time and spend it with Me
in the early hours of the morning
when all is new and fresh

and before the day has any blemishes.

Always start the day aright with Me,
then you will find it so much easier
to carry on for the rest of the day.

There are so many little things
to throw you off your course during the day.
You need a chart to refer to when this occurs,
and this is where time spent with Me
in the early morning
becomes invaluable;
when you learn to listen to that still, small voice
which is Mine
and record what I have to say.

Then when things become very difficult during the day,
and you realise that you are off course,
you can immediately refer to the chart
and put yourself on course again
without going round and round in circles
wasting precious time and energy.

You will always find that what you read at this time
has something in it
which you may not need right at this moment,
but sometime during the day
it will be brought to your conscious mind
and you will draw comfort and succour from it.

Never try to remember what you have read
but know that it will be tucked away
in your subconscious mind
to be drawn out when it is needed.

This is what happens to all you are learning at this time;
not a moment is wasted,

it is being stored away,
it is becoming absorbed into you;
and when you really need it
you will find it has become so much part of you
that it comes out automatically.

So every moment spent in reading something,
studying something,
is of the greatest value.
Be not depressed because you find you cannot remember
what you have read
from one moment to the next;
you are absorbing what you need for the future.

Slowly but surely great riches are being stored
in the back of the mind.
Keep constantly drawing on those riches;
they are not deposited there to be dormant
but to be used whenever necessary.

What is the use of having money in the bank
and yet you find yourself starved and destitute?
It is there to be drawn on and used,
therefore use it wisely.

So with all these precious jewels of wisdom
which have been deposited in your subconscious mind;
keep drawing out and using them,
leaving room for yet more to be stored until needed.

Remember I am limitless.
My gifts are all yours,
therefore your supply is limitless
be it wisdom,
be it love,
be it material needs.
All are yours

when you accept the wonder of our oneness
and glory in it.

As you read through these messages I have given you,
you realise what wonderful teaching
is contained in those written words
for learning to move into the new
and live in the new.
Only too often you write and write
because I tell you to do so,
but what you have actually written
means so very little to you;
and yet looking back at it
you realise what priceless gems are hidden there.

It is their very simplicity which makes them such gems.
Those teachings will be used by many in the days ahead
to help them,
to lift them,
to instruct them.
This will simply open up.
Just keep on your toes
and gradually things will be made clear.

You have always considered what I have given you
applied to the now,
for that specific day;
and so it does.
But it can also apply to any time
with anyone who is seeking for the answer
to a specific problem.

It is all there
contained in My words,
simple enough for a child to understand,
never cloaked in mystery or in parables.

Those who consider them too simple or childlike
suffer from spiritual superiority;
but those who recognise them for what they are
and accept them as the Truth
have indeed had their eyes opened
and walk in true humility and understanding.

It would help you
to go back every now and again
and read what has been given you by Me.

You say it makes you feel such a failure.
Maybe.
But it will also help you to see
My infinite love and patience,
and seeing that will make you want to do better,
to really try to live and practise what I keep telling you.

It will help you to realise how many times I pick you up
when you have fallen into the mire
and I have cleansed and set you on your feet again.
It will enable you to see
that when I have set My hand upon a soul
I will not let go.
I am with you always;
become ever conscious of Me in everything you do.

107

Live, live, live all I am teaching you.
Make My word live in your daily living.
Take action when action is called for.
Be very still when stillness is called for.

Read and re-read what I have to say to you each day
and then see that you not only take it to heart
but live it,
practise it,
vibrate with it.

When I say, 'Be at peace,'
or 'Be still and know that I am God',
are they just words to you,
lovely, comforting words?

Do you find yourself surrounded with that peace
so that nothing disturbs you?
Do you find yourself being perfectly still,
and find the truth in those words, 'I am God'?
They are such tremendous words,
the most powerful words that were ever spoken.

When you realise they are living words,
when you fully realise the power of those words,
you will find that you have reached and know
              the meaning
of having dominion over all things.
As you repeat those words over and over again
they become part of you.

You find that when you are very disturbed or restless
and you repeat to yourself, 'Be at peace, be at peace',
slowly a sense of peace begins to spread over you;
and the more you go on saying it
the more you feel yourself become one with that peace.

Repetition is a good thing
and very necessary
until you finally have absorbed a certain truth
and it has become a part of your living—
which you will find is what eventually happens.

So when you find I am repeating Myself to you
over and over again,
do not become impatient
but realise that I do this
because you have not yet absorbed fully
what I am telling you,
that the words have not yet become living words to you
and you have not started to vibrate with them.

I have infinite patience
and I will never cease from bringing home My truths
          to you
until finally they are a part of you
and you are living them all the time
in your daily life.

I have set My hand upon you,
I have chosen you to do a specific work for Me,
therefore I will not let you go.

Very patiently,
very lovingly,
I go on and on instructing you,
leading you,
guiding you.

I know your deepest longing is to do My will,
and that is one of the greatest steps in the right direction.
As long as you have that desire to do My will
I can always reach you.

I tell you from time to time
that time is getting short
and there is much to be done,
that time must not be wasted in doing unguided things,
that everything you do must be done with My blessings.

Take all this to heart
even though you do not quite know
what I mean by time;
at least let this knowledge keep you ever alert
and on your toes
so you live fully in the now
giving of your very best,
following out My instructions to the letter.

No one knows what tomorrow may bring,
therefore live to the full in the glorious now.

As you search diligently
you will surely find what you are looking for:
your at-one-ment with Me
the source of all life
all good;
but you have to take time to search.

This is something that will not drop into your lap
without the deep desire in you to know Me,
to know the truth,
to seek until you find what this really means to you.

This deep spiritual experience of inner knowing

comes only to those who really want to know.
Therefore never just dabble vaguely
in these spiritual experiences;
realise that once you have started on this quest
nothing will satisfy you
until you have found what you are looking for,
your at-one-ment with Me.

This is something each individual has to do on
            their own.
Someone may be able to point the way to you,
but it is up to you to do the rest,
it is up to you to go forth
and experience it within.

Until you start to put what you are learning into practice,
you really do not know whether it works for you or not.
It may work for others,
but what about you?
What does it mean to you to live by faith
unless you do something about it
and put it to the test?

Remember you cannot bask
in someone else's deep inner spiritual experiences.
It helps to read about them,
to learn about them
and even to hear and talk about them;
but it is up to you to live them
and practise them in your own life
if you desire to live by the spirit,
to live by faith.

You all know this
but what are you doing about it?
Are you just hearers of the word,
or are you doers of it?

No one can make you live this life;
every soul is absolutely free
to make its own choice.
What have you chosen?

Just to sit back
and spend the rest of your life
listening to other people's experiences?
Or are you going to start right here and now
living a life fully dedicated to Me,
to My work,
putting into practice all those wonderful lessons
you have been learning,
and seeing how they really do work?

How completely empty and futile life is
until you start living it to the full
and putting everything to the test
to see whether this spiritual life really is practical
and worth living.

Start right now doing something about it,
waste no more time talking about it;
there is far too much talk
and not nearly enough action.

Let there be no armchair spirituality;
let it be living,
and vibrating,
there for all to see.
Let Me see you start living a life *now*.

112

When you are in tune,
in harmony with all life
you will find that nothing can harm you
because you blend in perfectly with the whole
and you are master of the whole situation.

It is when you are out of harmony
and there is resistance in you
that you become the slave
and therefore open yourself up to negative forces.

In fact,
it is that which you fear that you draw to you
and become overwhelmed by.

Fear nothing.
There is nothing to fear when you are at one with all life.
That is why I constantly remind you
to be ever aware of Me
and of My divine presence.
When your whole being is filled with light and love
there is no room for any negativity;
for light and darkness cannot abide together
any more than love and fear.
Perfect love casts out all fear.

Whatever you undertake,
no matter how seemingly impossible
or heavy the task may be,
do it fearlessly
with the knowledge that you are not doing it on
        your own
but that I am with you always.
I will show you the way
and show you exactly how to handle the whole situation
so that it will fall into place and work out perfectly.

Never allow any doubts in
and never look back.
Simply know that what you have undertaken is right
and that only the very best will come out of it.
Go ahead in faith
and do what you know has to be done
and see perfect results.

How can you expect things to go right
and to go smoothly
when you are full of doubts
and riddled with fear?
You immediately put up a barrier
creating the wrong conditions
so bringing about failure.
It is all your own doing,
so never look around for a scapegoat to blame
but look within yourself
and recognise where you have gone wrong
and then do something about it.

Never be satisfied to wallow in your failures and
            mistakes
and be dragged down by self pity.
Miserable are those who are sorry for themselves
and allow self pity to creep into their life
and dominate it.

See your mistakes and failures;
learn by them,
be determined not to make the same mistakes again,
then move on;
giving thanks
for all the wonderful things life has endowed you with:
for life, for health,
for beauty all around you,
for friends, for the very breath you breathe,

114

for everything,
everything.
Realise more and more how mightily blessed you are
and how much you have to be grateful for.
As you do so,
all feelings of self and self pity
will disappear completely,
because your heart is full of love and gratitude
and you are in tune with Me
and all is very, very well.

Unite, unite, unite.
When there is unity
there is nothing to hold up the manifestation
of that which is on the etheric
and it can be brought about at great speed.

Search your hearts.
Is there anything in any of you
which is causing disunity and division,
which is holding up the manifestation
of the next phase of the work?
Is there any misunderstanding,
jealousy, envy,
or anything negative
which may be putting on the brakes?

This is something each one of you will have to seek
and find out deep within.
It is not something to be discussed or pulled to pieces.
It does mean that all will have to face themselves

fairly and squarely
and really be honest with themselves.
You will know without a shadow of doubt
if you happen to be that piece of grit
which is holding up the perfect outworking of My plan.

When you have faced up to it
you can do something about it:
you can seek My cleansing and purifying
and once again get into tune and harmony with
        the whole
and find that unity and oneness.

Do not sit back
and point your finger at anyone else;
simply take time to be still
and in the stillness look within your own heart.
If you find a great sense of peace and harmony within
you have nothing to be concerned about;
but if you feel uncomfortable
and find yourself making excuses
and trying to justify your actions and your thoughts,
you may be sure there is something deep within you
that needs to be changed.

When you recognise this
do not allow it to concern you and weigh you down
but start right there and then
to change your whole outlook and attitude.

I am always there to help you;
do not try to do it on your own.
Call on Me
and I will answer you
and help you to overcome
all that seems to stand in your way
preventing you from feeling at one with the whole.

There is so much on the etheric
which is waiting to be manifested in form on the
          physical;
wonder upon wonder,
miracle upon miracle.
Again I say,
unite and help to bring this about
without any further delay.
Allow nothing in you to hold it up.
Let not a thought of the self
or of what you want for the self
mar the plan.

Think only for the whole,
plan for the whole,
work for the whole,
give to the whole
and so help really to speed things up.

The perfect plan is there—
you help to bring it about.

Let Me fill your heart,
mind, soul and being
with the beauty and harmony of all life.
It is there all around you
and within you.

Wake up to it,
wake up
and enjoy it to the full

and give eternal thanks for it.

A life filled with beauty and harmony
is a joy to behold;
it radiates and projects
law and order
and perfect rhythm and harmony.

A true work of art
whatever it may be,
must have balance, grace,
harmony and order.
A beautiful soul reflects these qualities for all to see.
Have I not told you many times
that that which is within is reflected without?

When there is chaos and confusion within
it is reflected without
by a life of chaos and confusion
and it cannot be hidden.
So with peace, harmony,
beauty, love—
they are reflected in your outer living and appearance.

To get into rhythm with life
you have to learn the art of being still.
The stiller you can become
the clearer can you reflect the qualities of your soul.

How easy it is to blame your environment,
your situation,
your conditions
for the state you are in.
How nice it is to have something or someone else
        to blame,
to have a scapegoat.
It is high time you ceased doing this

and realised that you have only yourself to blame
for the state you are in,
that when you can seek and find
that inner peace and stillness
nothing and no one without will be able to disturb it
or throw you off balance.

Look around you,
look at the beauty and perfection of nature:
everything in nature is in rhythm,
there is perfect law and order in My universe,
nothing is out of tune,
there is a time and reason for everything.
It is all there for all to see
and for all to partake of,
so get into tune with it,
flow with it
and be part of that law and order in My universe.

Are you not part of the whole?
Then why separate yourself
by living a disordered, chaotic life?
As you fill your mind with beautiful thoughts,
say beautiful words
and accomplish beautiful things,
so do you become one with the beautiful wholeness
which is My universe,
which is Me
and everything fits in perfectly.

Take time to reflect on this,
and get into tune,
and into harmony,
and do it now.

As each individual seeks and finds
that inner peace and harmony

so will peace and harmony reign in the world.
It has to start somewhere;
so why not let it start in you,
and realise that you,
by doing your part,
can help to bring peace and harmony into the world.

It is every tiny drop of water that makes up the
                    mighty ocean;
and every tiny grain of sand that makes up the beach;
so every individual at peace within
can bring peace without into the world.
So why not do your part?

Expand your consciousness
and know that I am all there is.
Then go on and on expanding it
and see the all-inclusiveness of the I AM
and see clearly that you are the I AM of the I AM,
that there is no place where I am not.

Keep stretching,
feel every atom in you ache with stretching,
feel yourself growing,
breaking all bonds which have held you in bondage
and have stifled your growth and expansion.

As a tiny seed planted in the earth breaks its outer skin
and begins to grow
and expand
and develop into that which it really is,

so let your real self grow and expand
until you become what you really are
and behold the beauty and wonder of it all.

As you do so
know that you are one with all life,
now and forever;
that never again can you be separated from this,
that I am in you
and you are in the I AM.

As you take time in the stillness
and allow this to be absorbed into your being
to become a very part of you,
you will begin to find a new freedom in life,
you will begin to really live and move and have
            your being
in the wholeness of the whole,
you will find yourself in your true environment.
You will be able to do all things,
you will know that absolutely nothing is impossible
for it is the I AM who is working in and through you,
and when I am recognised
and accepted
anything is possible.

Can you feel yourself expanding now?
Can you accept all that I am saying to you?
Or are you still full of doubts and fears,
afraid to step out into the unknown,
to accept the truth
and know that the truth will set you free?

I can keep on imparting these wonderful truths to you,
but unless you are willing to accept them
and use them in your life and living
they will do you no good.

They improve with constant use.

What are you going to do about them?
It is up to you to take action.
You must have faith,
for know you not
that according to your faith be it unto you?
You must believe,
for without belief
you hold up the manifestation
of all My good and perfect gifts
which I am holding out to you.
Unless a gift which is held out to you
is accepted with grace and gratitude
it cannot benefit you.
Therefore let not pride or false humility
stop you from accepting
that which is your rightful heritage.

All that I have is yours
when you can accept your oneness with Me,
without any reservations.
Do this in that risen state of consciousness
where you know the truth of the I AM within you.

When you listen to My voice
it is the most natural thing in the world to you.
It has become as natural to you as breathing;
there is no strain about it whatsoever.
That is the way I want it to be.

It should never be necessary for you
to come into a special state
before you can hear My voice.
You should be able to hear it at all times and in all places
no matter what is happening around,
no matter what state you may be in—
your need for Me is constant.
As it was in the beginning
when people walked and talked with Me,
so it is happening again now.

Think on these things.
This is the most wonderful relationship
any soul could ask for,
and this, I want you to know, anyone can have.
This is the relationship I long to have with all
        My children.

Only the lower self prevents this happening.
You know this,
because if there is ever a blockage between us
it is never anything to do with Me.
I never withdraw Myself from My children.
They withdraw themselves from Me
by allowing the lower self to step into the way.

Each of you functions in a different way;
therefore never compare,
keep your heart open,
and your understanding,
and seek Me at all times.

Listen to the birds
singing My songs of praise,
and let your heart be full of joy and thanksgiving
and sing My praises forever.

My works are mighty.
My ways are wonderful.
Let Me work in and through each one of you.
Cooperate with life,
go with it
and do not fight against it.

Beyond all else, learn to get your values right
and put first things first.
I have told you many times
you cannot expect everything to drop straight into
            your lap
unless you do your part and put first things first.
It is time you learned this lesson,
for it is a fundamental one.

Stop for a moment in all your busy-ness
and see what you are putting first:
Is it work?
Is it living?
Is it your wants?
Your desires?
'Seek ye first My kingdom.'
Get into tune with Me,
find your direct contact with Me
and all else shall be added unto you.

Do you not realise that your communion with Me
means far more than anything else?
For it is from this contact that all else stems.

124

I am the source,
and until you realise this,
accept it,
and draw from it,
things do not happen.

You cannot draw water from a well
unless you get a bucket
and let it down on a rope into the well,
fill it with water
and then draw it up.
You have to do something,
you have to make the effort
and do your part.
Standing at the top of the well looking at the water
will not draw it up.

So with this spiritual life;
standing around
watching others using the laws of manifestation
will not make them work for you.
Seeing others find their oneness with Me
will not do it for you.

Every soul has to do its own inner seeking and finding.
All have to do their own inner work,
their own thinking,
make their own inner contact
and stand on their own feet.

No one can live on someone else's glory,
no one can live someone else's life for them.
You cannot be lazy spiritually,
you must do something about it.
Really see it work in your life and living.
It does work,
for all you have to do is to open your eyes

and you will see how truly wonderfully it works
in the lives of those who truly love Me
and put Me first in everything.

Why not take time to be still
and go into the silence,
study your motives
and see whether they are of the highest?

What are you doing
about the things that really matter in life?
Have you got your values right?
Only you can do this for yourself,
no one else can do it for you,
and it does take time and patience.
It may even mean waiting upon Me
without receiving an immediate answer.
You may have important lessons to learn
which you can only learn in this way
by being still
and waiting upon Me,
especially if you are an impatient and demanding soul.

Why make excuses for yourself?
You know all the answers in theory:
now it is time you put them into practice
and see how they work for you,
not just for others.

You will never learn these vitally important lessons
until you put them to the test.
Why not do it now
and stop wasting time thinking about them?

Be still,
be very still
and know that I am God,
that I am within you,
around you,
above you,
below you.

I am everywhere,
I am within all things.

Expand your consciousness.
Stretch until you ache all over.

Your deepest longing and desire
is to seek and find the truth;
therefore you cannot fail to do so
because as each soul chooses of its own free will to seek,
so will it find.
Every book you pick up to read
throws a little more light on what you are seeking.

You do not have to seek very far for the answer
for the answer lies within your very being.
You seek Me,
I am within.
You seek the truth,
the truth is within.
You seek joy and happiness;
that joy and happiness are not without,
again you will find them within.

You seek love,
that love is within.
All the treasures of heaven are within your very being.

Stop seeking,
but instead unlock the door
and step right into that world within
and there you will find all that you desire.
Nothing will be withheld from you,
for all is yours as soon as you become aware of it.

Is it not wonderful to know that your seeking days
           are over?
Now it is simply a case of unwrapping each gift
which you find within,
with the greatest of care,
studying each gift,
and then putting it to good use.

These gifts,
all of them,
are there to be used
and constantly used.

Never keep them to the self,
never hide them;
bring them forth and use them,
they improve with use.

As priceless pearls, when they are shut up in velvet
           caskets,
become sick from lack of wear
and have to be brought out into the light of day
and placed around someone's neck
to bring them to full life and glory again,
so with each gift.
Bring it out into the light so all can see, hide nothing.

You know you are one with Me;
therefore live that oneness,
demonstrate it in your everyday living.
Do not just display it on high days and holidays
but all the time.

You have within you the gift of My divine love;
let it shine forth in action.
There is no use talking about My divine love
if you do not live it
and demonstrate it in your living.

You feel happy;
well, let that happiness reflect in your whole being,
for that happiness stems from within.
Open the door and let it out.
You cannot say how happy you are
and then go around with a long face
and gloomy expression.
It must be expressed in your whole being.
Live happiness.

So with every gift you find within.
Unwrap it and put it to its full use.
That is the way you can live a full and glorious life,
that is the way you can demonstrate
that I am indeed one with you,
that I am indeed within you.
Let us live that life together and in complete
        at-one-ment.

SERVICE

I was shown a casket filled with wonderful jewels and precious stones.

Then I saw the lid snapped shut, the key turned in the lock, and the casket carefully put away into a very strong safe.

I heard the words: 'All My good and perfect gifts are there to be used, not to be put away for safekeeping. Why not open the doors of your heart, and use those gifts to My honour and glory.'

Step by step let the way open up,
with no feeling of strain or stress.
All is in My hands,
all has My blessings,
there is a pattern and plan
running through all that is happening.
Go ahead in absolute confidence,
and do what has to be done.

Keep your heart open so My divine love can pour
            through it.
Every soul needs to be assured of this.

Never feel you have nothing to give:
you have the most precious gift in all the universe
            to give
for you are a channel for My divine love.
Humanity is hungry for it,
the need in the world for it is tremendous.

You feel that it is so often misunderstood:
this is so.
But do not let this concern you.
You are My channel,
My instrument,
and as such you need only do My will.
Never concern yourself
regarding the reaction or effect it may have on anyone.

I ask you to say something,
to write something;

you obey My voice.
The outcome may be very different
to your own conception of what it ought to be.
Never mind.
Simply know and understand
that it is only when I have implicit obedience
to My word
that miracles can be brought about.
You simply do what I ask you to do
and then leave the rest to Me.

When a soul is ready I can work in them.
The seeds of love never fall on barren ground.
They may lie dormant for some time,
but eventually when conditions are ready
they will burst forth
and flower
and flourish.

So, you plant the seeds
and at the right time
I will tend those seeds.

All is very well.
The work that is being done here
is now bringing forth much fruit;
you will behold the wonder and glory of it
and will lift up your heart and glorify Me
and see My hand in all that has been happening.

It is a wonderful time,
a really thrilling time;
open your eyes and behold it
and realise that you are part of it.

It is not necessary to try too hard to become perfect;
simply hold before you the vision of My perfection
and know that that is what you are going to manifest
          in form,
perfection in all things;
for I am in all things
and I am perfection.

Blot out discord
and see only harmony all around you;
blot out imperfection,
and see only perfection.
You can do it
and you can do it instantly
without wasting any time wondering whether it
          is possible.

With Me all things are possible,
and I am within the very centre of your being.
I am that I am.
Vibrate from that tremendous statement,
and as you do so you raise your vibrations
and see the ordinary things in life
in a completely different light.
You begin to see a real sparkle
in something which you had always considered
so ordinary and mundane;
you begin to see life and purpose in everything
          around you;
you are living and vibrating in the new.

This is where life takes on a completely different hue;
instead of everything being just black and white
everything vibrates in colour.
You become very aware of colours,
you become very alert to the sounds
of nature all around you.
When you work in the garden
you become aware of tiny things
you have never noticed before.
You see in the work you are doing
a purpose, a lesson to be learnt.

You were pulling up nettles one day
and you wondered how you were going to tackle
a mass of them;
then you found as you tackled each little clump
as you came to it,
you were able to pull them up
and dispose of them quite easily.

You see how important it is to stop looking ahead
to just live fully in the moment
doing what is required of you in that moment.
That is the way to get on top of things.
If you try to look too far ahead
you become so overwhelmed
with the amount to be done
that you want to throw up your hands
and say, 'Impossible!'
that you are incapable of doing it.

That is why
by living fully in the moment
doing everything to the very best of your ability
you will be able to accomplish the seemingly impossible
without even realising that you are doing it;
and when you look back

and see what has been accomplished,
you will be amazed
and will lift up your heart in deep, deep gratitude
and give Me eternal thanks.

You will see My divine hand in everything
that has been accomplished
and know that indeed with Me
all things are possible.

Never try to undertake too many projects
for you simply waste your energy by spreading it
          too thinly.
When you do this
you are unable to do anything perfectly
or wholeheartedly
because when you are doing one thing
your mind is on the next.

This means you have not learned
that vital lesson of pinpointed concentration
which is what is essential
if you wish to create something.

Stop being a butterfly,
flitting from one project to the next,
never completing anything,
but learn the art of concentration
and of creation.

What are you really good at?

Search your heart
and find out
and then take that gift
and concentrate on it.

Are you good at music,
singing, acting?
Or is it painting or handicrafts?
Is it cleaning, or looking after people?

Whatever it is
and no matter how ordinary or mundane
it may appear to be,
learn to concentrate on it
and develop it.
Cease trying your hand at everything,
dissipating your power and energy
and failing miserably in everything as a result.

There are so many wonderful things to do in life
but realise right now
that you can only do one thing at a time;
so get on
and do one thing at a time
and do it wholeheartedly.

You will only be able to perfect what you are doing
if you practise.
You cannot hope to be a really good musician
unless you practise;
you cannot hope to be a good artist
unless you take time to practise your art;
you cannot hope to be a good mother and housewife
unless you put that into practice as well.

What can you do best?
Find out

and then go ahead and do it
and enjoy doing it.
Do not waste time and energy longing to do
            something else
or wishing you were somewhere else
with other opportunities.
Realise you are in exactly the right place at the right time
and you are there for a specific purpose
to do a specific job;
therefore give all you have got to that job
and do it with love and joy.

See what fun life can be
not just for yourself,
but also for all those with whom you are in contact.

What deep satisfaction you will find
when you do what has to be done perfectly
and when you do it for the benefit of the whole.
Unless you give of your very best to the whole
you cannot hope to become part of that whole,
you cut yourself off from it
and there is no wholeness in you.

Be yourself.
'To thine own self be true.'
When you are in contact with Me
and are drawing your all from Me,
your own self is your higher self,
never the lower self.
Then you can indeed be your true self

and live and work from a spiritual level of
        consciousness,
and behold the most amazing things taking place.
You will behold the supernatural things coming about
because you are working with My laws
and are in tune with all life.

As you learn to do this more and more
you will behold miracle upon miracle taking place
until you fully understand that with Me nothing is
        impossible.
But you must be true to that higher self.
You must be afraid of nothing
and be willing to do the most unusual things
without any hesitation.

Always remember that you are functioning from
        the spiritual,
not from the human level of consciousness.
You are working with My laws
not human laws;
and if these take you out on a limb
go out on it without a thought of self,
because you know that only the very best
        will come about.

Seek not approval
nor popularity with your fellows
but seek always to do My will
no matter what the cost.
This will not be easy for those who choose the easy way
and are determined to have peace at any price.
I tell you peace will come
and will be lasting
when it is sought by following out My directions,
even if at the time they may appear to be unreasonable
and even foolish.

When you choose to do My will
and walk in My ways
you have to do it wholeheartedly
no matter what this may mean.

You have to take the rough with the smooth
when learning the vital lesson
of instant obedience to My will.
Only when you give all
will you receive all.
In this spiritual life you cannot pick out all the plums
and leave the cake.
It is a case of all or nothing.

Many souls like to choose the parts in this life
that appeal to them
and to ignore those parts
that do not comply with their baser desires.
This is not living a spiritual life;
this is picking and choosing what you want to do,
not what I require of you.
You cannot expect things to work out for you
if that is your attitude.

I need your total surrender
and total dedication
before I can work
those wonders and miracles
in and through you.

You all know this;
so why not do something about it
and do it *now*?

'You shall know the truth and the truth shall set
        you free.'

Never at any time close your heart and mind;
never be afraid of the new,
of the strange,
of the unconventional.
Be ready and prepared to listen to the intuition,
to the inspiration,
which may reveal something completely new to you—
something so new
that it may not even have form or substance
and you may have to give it form and substance
and may have to clothe it in words.

Nothing is new in the universe,
but much has been hidden down the ages
which is now to be revealed.
It has been hidden because people have misused it
by using it for the self
and for self-glorification
so that all that wonderful wisdom, knowledge
        and power
has had to be withdrawn:
until people have learned to take nothing to the self;
until they have realised that they are nothing
and are willing to give Me the honour and glory
        for everything;
until they have recognised that it is I
working in and through them
which enables them to do the work.

142

Take nothing to the self
for as soon as you do that
you block the flow of inspiration
and I know immediately
when something is being drawn to the self.
Give constant praise and thanksgiving
for everything that is being revealed to you
and then go forth
and use it for the benefit of the whole:
realising that you are but My channel,
My messenger,
and that all you receive comes from Me.

You long for the joy and freedom
of the spirit:
it is yours
as soon as you accept
where all your good and perfect gifts come from,
and you acknowledge Me
as the source of your all,
and accept that you are as nothing without Me.

Intellectual pride can be a handicap
along this spiritual path
and can be a real stumbling block to the truth.
It is not the intellect you need,
it is inspiration and intuition.
The intellect comes from without,
whereas inspiration and intuition come from within
and cannot be influenced by anything without.

Let your learning come from within;
draw from all that you have within you.
You will be amazed at what you contain:
it is limitless
because it comes from Me and I am limitless
and all that is of Me is limitless and eternal.

143

Why not start drawing from that source right now?
Each one of you has this wonderful potential within you
but there it remains
until you choose to draw it forth
and use it in its right way.
Misuse any of My gifts
and they will be withdrawn from you.
Always remember this.

Bring down My heaven upon the earth;
it is up to you to do it.
It is up to you to create heaven upon the earth
by the way you live,
by your attitude towards life.

Life is wonderful
but you have to open your eyes
and see the wonder and glory of it.

You must be willing to see all the good things in life,
concentrate on them
and ignore the bad,
the negative,
the destructive things,
and give them no life force.

When I tell you to behold My new heaven and new earth
you have to do something about it.
They are there;
but few there are who are fully aware of them
and realise that they are there for all

144

not just for the select few to enjoy.
Unless you are aware of what is going on around you,
you cannot take part
and become part of it.

With the new come great changes,
and very often it is the changes
that you dislike,
with the result that you would prefer to remain
with your eyes tightly shut;
to stay in the old
and know nothing about the wonderful new heaven
and new earth
waiting there for you.

You only see what you want to see,
you remain blind to the rest.
You only hear what you want to hear;
all around you are the wonders and beauty of nature
and yet you can go through a whole day
without even noticing what is around you.

The tiny larks can be singing their songs of praise
as they soar higher and higher into the sky,
and yet you can be completely oblivious
to the wonder of their song
unless you take time to stop
and listen
and become aware of what is happening.

What a lot you miss in life
by simply shutting it out of your consciousness,
by refusing to raise your consciousness
to the state where you blend together with all life.

Take time to stop,
to look

and to listen
so that you miss nothing
and can really enjoy everything.
Then give eternal thanks for it all.

Start this day to create a better world around you
by all you do,
say and think
and really enjoy it all to the full.

Life is there to be enjoyed
and every day should be full to overflowing
with all the good things in life.
Expect the best
and accept only the best.

You have been told this many times:
yet many of you are still content
to accept second best
either because you feel unworthy to receive the best
or you are just too lazy to raise your consciousness
until you visualise the very best
and then hold the very best in your consciousness
until it manifests in form.

This is where you have to put into practice that lesson
of patience,
persistence
and perseverance
and see it work out.

Give constant thanks for all My good and
            wonderful gifts
which I pour down upon you.
Use them all for the benefit of the whole
and to My honour and glory
and you will indeed find true and lasting happiness
and contentment.

By all means use them—
they have been given to you to use;
but do not let them use you,
do not become possessive of those wonderful gifts
and hold them to the self;
or you will surely lose them,
for they have been given to you
to give,
to share,
to delight in the sharing.

Every soul has something to share.
There are gifts and possessions on many different levels.
You may not have material gifts,
but you may be sure you have other gifts
whatever they are.

Hold them not to the self,
hide them not
but be willing to bring them out into the open,
uncover them
and then use them as they should be used:
never for the glorification of the self
but always to My honour and glory.

Possess nothing
but use and enjoy all you have to the full.
The gifts I give you are not given to be hidden away
but are there to be used.

What have you to give?
Take time to find out, if you do not know.
It may be something unique;
and because it is unique
you may feel it is not worthwhile sharing
because you cannot see how it can fit into the whole.
I tell you
every gift can be used
and should be used fully.

This is why you have all been drawn together in
            this way,
why you are all so different,
so that you can all become part of the perfect whole
as you contribute your specific gift,
and allow it to be used for the whole,
without a single thought of the self
or what you can get out of it.

Give wholeheartedly
and give with joy,
and be grateful that you have something to give,
whatever it may be.
It is not necessary to let your left hand know
what your right hand gives.
It is not necessary to shout about your gifts
but very quietly to give of them
and as you do so to see how they are needed
and how they fit in perfectly with the whole.

Be grateful for being used in this way.
When you have chosen to live this way of life
completely dedicated to Me and to My work,
you can no longer cling on to anything
because you realise that all you have is Mine
and therefore it is there to be shared with the whole.

How many times have you heard
or even muttered to yourself:
'What a mess the world is in these days!
What a state of chaos and confusion!'

You have felt that there was nothing much
you could do about it.
It seemed hopeless
and out of your control,
and you have hidden yourself away in your shell
like a snail,
and left the world to get worse and worse.

Where is your sense of responsibility
towards the state of the world?
Do you not realise:
that what you do,
how you live,
how you think
can help or hinder the state of the world?

It takes every tiny grain of sand to make up the
            sea shore;
it takes every tiny drop of water to make up the ocean.
What you do with your thinking
helps to make or mar the world;
have you ever thought of that?

The more souls who are thinking loving,
positive, constructive thoughts
about the world,

the more you realise
what a truly wonderful and beautiful world
you are living in.
You are all very much a part of it,
you are all a tiny part of that vast wholeness
and you have your specific part to play.
The more quickly you realise this
the sooner will the state of the world begin to change.

Cease being drawn into the whirlpool
of universal thoughtforms of chaos and confusion
of destruction and devastation.
Start right now concentrating on the wonder and beauty
of the world around you.

Give thanks for everything,
bless all those whom you contact,
refuse to see the worst in people,
in things,
in conditions
and seek always for the very best.
Concentrate on that very best
and see the wonderful changes
which will take place in the world
all around you.

You can do this
and you can start doing it today.
In fact you can start doing it now.

This is not being like an ostrich
hiding your head in the sand
and refusing to face the realities of the world;
it is simply looking for
and concentrating on
the very best in everything and everyone.

You are a tiny world within yourself.
When there is peace,
harmony,
love and understanding
right there, deep within your little world,
it will be reflected on the outer,
in the world all around you.

Start putting your own house in order,
start readjusting your thinking and living.
Stop pointing your finger at anyone else
and spotlighting their faults and failings.
You have more than enough to do to right yourself.
When you can do that
you are beginning to help
the whole vast situation in the world.

Why not start right now
really to love the world you are in,
really to enjoy it to the full,
to absorb the beauties and wonders of it?

It is full of energies, of goodness.
It is a wonderful, wonderful world
and you are greatly blessed and privileged
to be living in it.

It is up to you to bring down heaven upon earth.
What are you doing about it?
Stop looking to someone else to do something about it,
and start doing it yourself.

Don't be a hypocrite.
You cannot say you love Me
and hate your fellow humans
for love and hate are like oil and water—
they do not mix.

When you truly love Me
you will love your fellows;
you will love one another,
you will have compassion and understanding
towards one another.
And when you love one another
you will love Me—
they are so intertwined that they cannot be separated.

Love is so strong
yet so gentle.
None has greater love than the one
who lays down their life for a friend.
How great is your love for one another?
Are you willing to put yourselves out for one another?
Are you willing to go that second mile
no matter how busy or how weary you are?

Love does not need to be expressed in words,
it is seen and felt in action,
it radiates from you—
it *is* you.

Love is the language of silence,
it can be understood and accepted
without a word being spoken,
it is an international language
understood by the heart
not by the mind.

It matters not what nationality you are,

you can always convey love
and communicate it in complete silence.
Your eyes,
your heart,
your attitude,
your whole being
can convey what you are feeling towards one another.

When love flows freely in the hearts of all,
hatred, jealousy, war and dissent will be no more
and peace will reign supreme.
Without love there can be no peace,
no understanding.

You cannot learn about love from books,
you cannot be told about love.
You just have to *be* love
and open your heart
and let it flow.
Love stems from Me—
I am love.

Raise your consciousness,
forget yourself,
think of others,
give in service to others
and joy and love will radiate from you.
As you learn to give to others in service
it opens your heart
and keeps it open.

The more you give freely and joyously
the more love pours forth from you
and the more love you draw to you.

You cannot love without being loved;
it is a two-way thing—

a giving and a receiving.
The more love you give,
the more you will receive.
This is the law.

Never be discouraged
if love is not returned to you immediately.
Simply know that sooner or later it will be,
and just keep the love flowing
no matter what the response may be,
for love will melt the hardest of hearts in the end.

Love never takes 'no' for an answer.
Love is never defeated.
Love is not like a snail,
it never withdraws when it is rebuffed or rejected.
It turns the other cheek
and just goes on and on loving.

Can you do this?
You cannot do it in your own strength
but with Me you can do anything.
Seek My help at all times
and I will never fail you
and you will find you can love
and love
and go on loving
without any difficulty.

Your life is My life lived through you.
You are My hands and feet
and I need each one of you to work in and through.
You are all different aspects of the whole
and you are all greatly needed in your different ways.

Never withdraw yourself
feeling that you are not needed
and that someone else can take your place.

You each have something unique to contribute to
        the whole,
therefore let yourself be used.
Do your part, whatever it may be,
wholeheartedly
and find your rightful place
in the whole vast intricate pattern of life.

Give eternal thanks
that you can be used in that specific way
which is your own unique way.

Have you found out what you can contribute to
        the whole?
Can you feel yourself blending in, in true perfection?
Or do you still feel you are standing on the outside
looking in
wondering just where you fit in?
Why not step right in
and by so doing
find that special place more quickly and easily?
Once you are part of that whole
you will want to give of your very best.
You will want to find your place
and know exactly where you fit in.

Many times I have likened this to a clock with its
        many parts.

Every part is needed for the clock to go
and to keep the right time,
and it is when each part is in its rightful place
doing its specific job
that precision timing is achieved.

You cannot all be the face or the hands of the clock—
the parts that are in the forefront
and are seen all the time.
Those tiny screws and cogwheels are just as important—
those springs and parts that are tucked away
unseen by any except the clock mender
must be there for the clock to function.

Never try to be like someone else,
just be yourself
and do your part whatever it may be.
Be not resentful because you are in the background
tucked away unnoticed by the many.
Simply realise that in your own quiet way
you are greatly needed
for the smooth running of the whole.

Do all that you have to do with your whole heart
and really enjoy doing it.
Find real joy in seeing the smooth running of the whole
and know that you are doing your part
to help bring it about.

Every soul longs to be wanted,
to be really needed.
When you feel needed
you begin to grow
and to flower and flourish
and give of your very best.

Always remember that I have need of you;

so offer yourself anew to Me each day
that I can use you as I will,
and grow in strength and stature.

Shoulder your responsibilities joyously,
whatever they may be.
Life is a real joy,
wake up and realise this.
You are mightily blessed,
realise this too.

Take absolutely nothing for granted,
for when you do
life goes dead on you
and all the joy goes out of it.
Give constant thanks for everything
and really count those blessings.

Do what you know you have to do to My honour
and glory
and therefore do it perfectly.

'Do unto others as you would have them do unto you.'

No one likes to be hurt or slighted,
no one likes to be ignored
or made to feel unloved and unwanted.
So why not treat your fellow humans with love
and respect?
Try to understand them
and be willing to go that second mile with them if
necessary.

157

Be very tolerant,
very patient and very loving.
This is the way you would like to be treated yourself,
so live as you would wish others to live.

Be an example
and see that it is a really good example;
but never do it because you feel it is expected of you,
do it because you really want to do it,
and long with all your heart
to give of your highest and best
in everything you do, say and think.
The greater your desire
the easier it will be to fulfil it.

Never be satisfied with anything mediocre
or half-hearted.
See that everything you do is of the very highest,
that your motives are pure
and that there is nothing selfish or self-centred
in anything you do.

Take time to search your heart
and find out why you are doing what you are doing
and why you are where you are
and then answer yourself truthfully.

It is important at this time that you are in the right place
doing the right thing
for these are crucial times.
So much is taking place on many levels
and each soul is needed in its rightful place.
It is like a vast jigsaw puzzle being put together—
there is a right place for every tiny piece.

Are you in your rightful place?
Only you will know.

Do you feel comfortable with the vibrations?
Do you feel you blend in perfectly with the whole:
that you do not create any jarring or discordant note,
doing what you are doing
and living where you are living?

You must be prepared for a tremendous release of light
and if you are not prepared
it will throw you off balance.

Peace, harmony, tranquillity
must be within you,
to stabilise you
and bring you into alignment
with what is about to take place.

Therefore it is necessary to be still
and find that peace within
so that nothing and no one can disturb it.
Hold on to it no matter what is taking place without.

Be like an anchor,
strong and steady,
sunk deep within,
immovable so that no storm without
can affect you
or shift you from your rightful place.

Hold fast,
and know that all is very, very well,
that all is proceeding according to My perfect plan.

How wondrous are My ways;
walk in them
and know that no harm can befall those who do so.

Let not your heart be troubled

but put your whole trust, faith and security in Me
and go your way in peace,
doing what you know has to be done.
Let Me guide and direct your every step.

You are all members of one body,
all parts of the whole,
and each of you
has your part to play in the whole.

Be not critical
nor intolerant of one another;
but realise that no two of you are the same,
nor have you all the same function,
that it takes many different parts
to make up the perfect whole.

Have you ever seen a clock taken to pieces?
There are many different parts that make up that clock;
and as you see them lying there before you
you wonder how they could ever make up
a perfect timepiece.

But when someone who knows something about clocks
takes each piece
and puts it in its rightful place
you find that not only does it go
but it tells the correct time.
As long as each tiny piece remains in its rightful place
playing its part,
everything goes smoothly.

Now you know why it is that I keep telling you
to find your rightful place in the whole vast scheme
        of life
and when you have found it,
to give of your very best.
Do not waste time pulling your neighbours to pieces
and finding fault with them;
you really have more than enough to do
to keep yourself on the straight and narrow path
without finding fault with others.

There are so many different paths to the centre,
and when all are headed in the same direction
they must be right.
All must feel free to tread the path of their own choosing
and none should be pushed into one
that does not appeal to them.

All souls have free will.
What they do with that free will is up to them.
They can direct it into the light
and follow the light,
or they can choose the way of darkness
and grope their way in that.
It is simply up to each individual.

That divine spark is within each individual
but it needs to be drawn out
and fanned into a flame in so many souls.
It has to be recognised before anything can be done
        with it.
Wake up from your slumbers,
recognise the divinity within you;
nurture it
and allow it to grow and flourish.

A seed has to be planted in the soil before it can grow.

It has within it all its potential,
but that potential remains dormant
until it is given the right conditions
in which to grow and develop.

You each have within you the kingdom of heaven;
but unless you wake up to the fact
and start searching for it
you will not find it,
and there it will remain.

There are many souls in this life
who will not wake up to this fact,
and they are like seeds stored away in packets.
You must want to break your bonds,
to be free.
As soon as the desire is there
you will receive help in every possible way;
but the desire in you must be there.

Can you accept that you have within you
all power,
all wisdom,
all understanding?
Or is this still theory to you?

Are you still just hearers of My word but not doers?
Do you really want to be a power in the world,
do you want to be able to help and uplift?

Then you must learn to be true

to the very highest within you.
You will not only have to accept but know
without a shadow of doubt
that I am within you
and that I can do all things.
Nothing is impossible with Me
and with this inner knowing
you can be master of every situation
and rise above anything that would stand in your way.

Learn to act from that inner voice
and do not allow yourselves to be influenced
by outer conditions
or by those around you.
It is so much easier to follow the crowd
rather than follow your own individual path
knowing that it is right for you.
It needs inner strength and conviction
to enable you to do this,
and this is something each individual will have to seek
and find within themself.

Never be pig-headed and obstinate—
that is not being strong and confident,
acting from that inner knowing and conviction;
it is simply trying to assert an outer power and authority
which leads to dictatorship and slavery
and no good can come out of that.

When you know that something is right for you
there is no need to try and convince anyone or yourself;
but be strong and of good courage,
go ahead doing it very quietly and unobtrusively
allowing nothing and no one to try and turn you
            off course.
Retain that perfect balance deep within,
then nothing can touch you.

Draw from the infinite source of power and strength
        within,
and you will find yourself
doing seemingly supernatural things
simply because you are working with My divine laws.

When you are doing that, anything can happen
for My laws are the keys that open all doors
and make all things possible.

Recognise them as My laws
and never fail to give eternal thanks for them
and use them to My honour and glory
and for the benefit of the whole.
Then only the most wonderful things
can come out of their right use
and all shall benefit from them.

Power used aright under My guidance
can change the course of history,
creating the new heaven and the new earth,
bringing life,
life,
and more life.

Used wrongly it can bring only devastation and
destruction.

Power is something that must not be played with
but must be treated with great respect;
the way you respect the power of electricity
which can be a great help and benefit when used aright,
but when wrongly used can destroy and bring
        devastation.

164

I am power.
I hold all creation in My hand
and you are all part of that whole.
Blend with it
and find your rightful place in it.

I am the first and the last,
the beginning and the end.
I am in everything and everyone.
There is nowhere where I am not.
Tune in to the I AM of the universe
and be at one with all life
and start doing it now.

Be of one heart,
one mind,
one spirit.

Find perfect peace and harmony within
and reflect it without.
Peace starts within.
It is there within every soul
like a tiny seed
waiting to germinate,
and grow,
and flourish.
It has to be given the right conditions,
the right environment,
the right treatment
before it can start doing this.

Be still and create the right conditions;
be still and give it a chance to take root.
Once it is established it will continue to grow,
but in its tender beginnings it needs to be helped
and cherished.

You hold the key to world peace within,
therefore start using that key correctly right now.
It is stiff
and the lock is rusty from lack of use;
pour the oil of love into it
and start to turn it.
It may take time to lubricate it so that it can turn
            with ease,
but the more love it gets
the more easily it will turn.

Do not waste time
looking at the chaos and confusion in the world
but start putting it right within yourself.
Quietly go about doing My will.
You do not have to talk about it but simply live it.
Transform the chaos and confusion in your own life
to peace, serenity, tranquillity
and become a useful member of society
and the world you live in.
Start with yourself
where you know you can do something,
and then work outward.

Far too many souls waste time and energy
blaming the wrongs in the world on to everyone else
instead of recognising that they can do something
            about it
when they start within themselves.
Start putting your own house in order first,
then you can help your neighbour.

When a stone is thrown into the centre of a pond,
the ripples go out and out
but they start from that stone,
they start from that centre.
Start with yourself,
then you can radiate
peace, love,
harmony, understanding
out to all around you.

Go into action now;
there is no better time than the present.
You long to see changes,
then start changing yourself.
You long to see a better world, a better society,
then do something about it
not by pointing your finger at everyone else
but by looking within;
searching your own heart,
righting your own wrongs,
finding the answer within yourself.
Then you can move forward, with authority,
and be a real help to your neighbour,
and to all those you contact.

Change starts with the individual,
goes out into the group,
the community,
the town,
the nation,
the world.
Wholeness within creates wholeness without.
Seek and find that wholeness,
that oneness,
that union with all life;
as you seek you will find
for you will find Me in everything
and great will be the rejoicing.

Learn to appreciate and really care for all
that is given to you.
Learn to be good stewards
of all My good and perfect gifts.
You will only do this when you learn
to take the whole on your hearts
and realise that all you have comes from Me.
Therefore you long to cherish and care for everything.

When living in a community
this is a vitally important lesson to learn
and yet a very difficult one,
especially when you fail to shoulder your responsibilities
as they should be shouldered.

Realise that until those important lessons
of caring for and looking after all I have given you
have been learned
no more will be given.

Freely do I give to you
but stewardship of all I give you is essential.
This means that your attitude towards everything
          that is here
must be right,
that nothing is taken for granted,
that there is no demand in any of you,
that each of you learns to look after everything that
          you use,
from the smallest thing to the biggest;
that when something needs mending or maintenance

you personally see that it is done
and do not just leave it for someone else to do
and shelve your responsibilities.
If you cannot do it yourself,
find the right person to do it and ask for their help.

Take time to ponder on your attitude
towards everything you have
and everything you are given:
very often when something is easily obtained
adequate care is not given to it
and real care is not taken
because you do not feel it belongs to you personally.

This attitude has to change,
especially as you live in a community.
What you have comes from Me,
it is a gift from Me, your Beloved.
When you truly love the giver
you will really cherish the gift.
When you fail to look after My gifts
it reflects your attitude towards Me
the giver of all those gifts.

Love is the key to all this:
love for Me,
love for the whole,
love for each other,
love for everything.
When you really know the meaning of love
you will never again fail to love and care for all your
            charge.

You do not give a child a valuable piece of equipment
to play with
because you know that child will not look after it
and will probably destroy it.

I cannot give you all that is waiting to be given to you
until you learn to look after it
and use it the way it should be used—
with love and care.

Therefore I have to wait patiently until you are ready
before I can give you more and more of My gifts.

I have told you many times
that all My good and perfect gifts are yours,
in fact that all I have is yours;
but I have always added:
'When you have learned to love Me
and put Me first in everything.'
I say this because only then will I know
that you will really look after everything
the way it should be looked after.

NUTSHELLS

Joy
great joy I bring you this day
as you watch My perfect pattern unfold
like a glorious flower in the rays of the sun;
leaf by leaf you will behold its beauty and its perfection,
and you will lift up your heart to the true glory of it
and sing a song of deep praise and glory
and thanksgiving for all you see.

There is something tremendous happening at this time
and you are part of what is happening.

You are one of the actors in the play
and you must be ready to take your part
when you get your cue.

Seek within and you will find the answer.
Truth is like a many-sided diamond:
every side belongs to the whole
but it all depends where you are
as to just how you view it.
Every soul views truth from a different angle.
There is a time along the pathway of every soul
when it has to stand alone before Me
and find the I AM within
with no help or guidance or support from anyone else.

I want you to stop for a moment
and think of a butterfly
emerging from the comfort and security of its chrysalis.
Supposing the butterfly stopped in its process
        of emerging
and said:
'No, I cannot leave this place,
I don't know what lies outside this place.'
Suppose it stopped and refused to move out.
What would happen?
It would be failing in its own evolution,
and if it remained in its chrysalis
it would simply shrivel up and die.

So with you!
To refuse to move on
because you are afraid of the unknown
would most certainly hold up your evolution.

Love opens up a new world around you.
When you love, your vision expands and is magnified.
When you look at a flower with love,
you see the true beauty of it;
it is not just a flower
but part of My wonderful creation,
part of the whole.
You know the meaning of Oneness.

Every time you stop and say 'Thank you, Beloved,'
you are aware of Me.
Every time you behold the beauties of nature
and you glory in them,
you are aware of Me.
Every time you feel your heart opening up
and love flowing to a soul,
you are aware of Me.

Raise your consciousness continually
until you are ever conscious of Me and of My presence
and you really understand
that I am within the very centre of your being,
that there is no separateness,
that we are One;
and then never let your consciousness stray away
from that awareness.

There has to be a complete working in harmony
with each of you.
No player can become 'bolshie' in an orchestra
allowing personal likes and dislikes towards the
conductor to come in and because of these personal
feelings throw down their instrument
and refuse to play.

That is why perfect understanding is necessary
to create perfect harmony
and all the personal must go.
This is a fact
and it will be achieved
but it means a real stretching on all your parts to
            achieve it.

It is practice that makes perfect.
Without practice
you will be unable to perfect anything.
A musician has to practise
and practise
to reach concert standard;
an artist has to practise
to reach professional standard;
an athlete has to practise
to reach Olympic standard;
therefore to reach a perfect spiritual life
you have to live a life
and practise it
day in
and day out.

Every organ in the body has its rightful place,
and when it is functioning as it should
the body is whole and perfect.
Every soul has a rightful place
in the whole scheme of things,
and as each one gives what it has to give to the whole
the work moves forward in true perfection
and there is harmony and beauty and rhythm
everywhere.
Live for the whole,
think for the whole,
give to the whole,
work for the whole;
so feel part of the whole and become part of it
that there is no separation.
All is working in perfect unison and harmony.

Find your own path
and tread it with absolute faith and confidence.
It is foolishness to try and walk in someone else's
    footsteps
and try to imitate them in what they are doing.
Until you know your own special path
you will try one path after another—
seeking,
seeking,
always seeking;
but when you eventually find your path
nothing and no one will be able to turn you from it
and that path will carry you to the ultimate goal:
your realisation of oneness with Me.

Take time this day to be still
and find out what you have to give.
Realise it takes all sorts to make the whole.

It takes all the tiny screws and cogs and springs
to make a watch,
and every tiny piece has to fit into its place perfectly
and has to work with precision;
one thing out of alignment
and the whole thing is thrown out.

See that you all fit into your rightful places
and work perfectly
and in harmony and rhythm.

Real joy comes from giving
and finding your rightful place.

Far too many souls are satisfied to sit down
and accept what others have to say
instead of seeking for the truth within themselves.
They prefer to read and study other teachings
instead of finding those spiritual truths
            and teachings
deep within themselves.

Every soul is the microcosm of the macrocosm.
Every soul has all it needs deep within.

Start right now
drawing from that infinite eternal source
which knows no beginning and no end.

It is only as you practise living in My presence,
as you take time to be alone with Me
and listen to My still, small voice
and obey it
that you begin to understand
the wonder of your oneness with Me,
and you begin to bring down My heaven upon earth
for all to see.
Talking about it does not do it,
living and demonstrating it does.

A tiny spark can start off a tremendous blaze.
A small thing shared with another soul
can bring light and comfort
where there was only darkness and despair.

Act on those promptings which come from within
and never hesitate
for they may be that tiny spark
which will ignite something
within a soul in very great need.

Release love into every situation
and see what happens.
To release love:
you have to fill your consciousness
with loving,
positive,
constructive thoughts;
you have to transform every seeming negative situation
into a positive one—
but do it quickly.

When you see a plant wilting and dying for lack of water
and you immediately give it a drink
you can see a change in it straight away.
So with relationships:
when you see them strained and wilting
apply immediately the water of My divine love
and watch a complete transformation take place.